W9-BML-771

MANNERISM—STYLE, AND MOOD:

AN ANATOMY OF FOUR WORKS

IN THREE ART FORMS

MANNERISM—

STYLE

AND MOOD

An Anatomy of Four Works in Three Art Forms

by Daniel B. Rowland

New Haven and London: Yale University Press, 1964

Acknowledgment is made to the following sources:
The Johns Hopkins Press, for permission to use the text of "Astrophel"
as published in *The Works of Edmund Spenser*, Volume 1, and for permission to use the text of "The First Anniversary" as published in *John
Donne: The Anniversaries*, edited by Frank Manley.
Louis L. Martz, for permission to use the text of "On the Assumption"
as published by Doubleday and Company, Incorporated, in *The Medita-
tive Poem.*

To Joseph T. Curtiss

YALE COLLEGE SERIES

The tradition of undergraduate writing and publishing has long been a very lively one at Yale, as witnessed by the large number of periodicals, journalistic or literary in character, which have appeared on the Yale campus. These, however, fail to give an accurate picture of the high proportion of good and original scholarly writing which is also done by undergraduates. The excellence of many of the Honors theses written by Yale Seniors made it desirable some years ago to give the most deserving of them the circulation which publication in printed form could provide. Between 1941 and 1957 ten volumes were published in the Undergraduate Prize Essays Series and two in the Scholars of the House Series. The authors of several of these essays have gone on to fulfill amply the promise of their early scholarly efforts. More recently the growing number of theses of outstanding merit has encouraged Yale College and the Yale University Press to establish this new Yale College Series with the hope that every year it will be possible to publish some of the best work by the Honors majors in the Senior Class. The selection, which is necessarily a very rigorous one, was performed for the Class of 1963 by a faculty committee made up of Messrs. A. S. Foord, S. W. Reed, and E. M. Waith, Chairman.

Georges May
Dean of Yale College

PREFACE

This book deals with Mannerism in various art forms. As such it is speculative and even provocative, likely to arouse strong feeling, since there are those who instinctively condemn correlations among the arts. Furthermore, the very concept of Mannerism itself is ill-defined and controversial. To what purpose, then, can we seek to introduce a new and untried concept into fields which have done quite well without it?

Although Mannerism is a fairly well-established concept in the history of art, in music it may be said to have taken only reluctant root, and in literature it is practically ignored. With respect to art history, Sydney J. Freedberg sums up clearly the present condition of published knowledge about Mannerism in the preface to his study of the Mannerist Parmigianino:

> The serious and intermittently intensive investigation of the art-historical phenomenon of Mannerism began some thirty years ago. . . . [from this investigation] the broad outlines of a solution to the problem of Mannerism have emerged, and found a measure of general acceptance. However, these outlines are still vague; in a generation's research they have not yet assumed precise nor often even comprehensible form. The great bulk of our published knowledge in the field of Mannerism consists of generalizations, many of them acute, but others of remarkable looseness.
>
> The present need in our investigation of Mannerism is to specify these generalizations, and to give them some more concrete substance than the wide sampling of facts, or often fancies, on which they have been based.[1]

In my essay I have tried to meet this need while at the same time exploring the possibility of applying the term Mannerism to phenomena outside art history. To counteract the danger of superficiality inherent in such correlations, I have restricted the

1. Sydney J. Freedberg, *Parmigianino* (Cambridge, Mass., Harvard University Press, 1950), p. vii.

study to four works of art, two paintings, one madrigal, and one poem. My conclusions will therefore be firmly rooted in these particular works, each of which will be considered as a whole. This method will enable us to escape the dangerous process of sampling at random single aspects of various works. What has been lost in comprehensiveness I hope will be gained in depth and intensity.

There can be no valid correlation made among the arts unless all forms of art share some common elements. A perceptive statement of the essential unity of all the arts is found in the famous study of J. S. Bach by Albert Schweitzer:

> We classify the arts according to the material they use in order to express the world around them. One who expresses himself in tones is called a musician; one who employs colours, a painter; one who uses words, a poet. This, however, is a purely external division. In reality, the material in which the artist expresses himself is a secondary matter. He is not only a painter, or only a poet, or only a musician, but all in one. Various artists have their habitation in his soul. His work is a product of their cooperation; all have a part in each one of his ideas . . .
>
> Every artistic idea is complex in quality until the moment when it finds artistic expression. . . . Art in itself is neither painting nor poetry nor music, but an act of creation in which all three cooperate. . . . Every artistic feeling is really an act. Artistic creation is only a special case of the artistic attitude toward the world. . . . Art is the translation of the aesthetic associations of ideas. The more complexly and intensely the conscious and unconscious concepts and ideas of the artist communicate themselves to us through his art-work, the deeper is the impression. It is then that he succeeds in stimulating others to that vivacity of imaginative feeling which we call art, in contradistinction to what we hear and see and experience in our ordinary moments.[2]

For Schweitzer, art, the thing itself, does not reside in any particular discipline. The underlying "aesthetic association of

2. Albert Schweitzer, *J. S. Bach* (London, A. C. Black, 1923), 2, 8–15.

ideas" which is the very core of art transcends all disciplines and is prior to them. But one must always remember that the "languages" are merely outgrowths from this intangible aesthetic association. Art is not the language used; it is rather the transference of ideas into various kinds of language, and style, we might add, is the way in which each language is used. Or, in other words, style is the total effect produced by the way in which any artist uses the materials of his craft. If this be true, the historian who seeks a true understanding of style cannot limit himself to the bounds of one artistic medium; he should rather try to search out this underlying complex of ideas or attitudes which may find its expression in any or all of the various arts.

But what is this aesthetic association of ideas which art is to communicate? It is simply experience taken in its fullest sense. The reason why art may not be ultimately divided into disciplines is that the artistic experience itself does not consist of only colors, only tones, or only words. This experience consists of a whole set of sensations together with the emotional attitude brought to the work by the artist. Experience in this sense thus involves the interaction of an external stimulus, the sight of Tintern Abbey, for example, together with the emotional predispositions which the artist brings to the experience. The result is a peculiar mixture, an experience involving an association of all kinds of diverse ideas, visual as well as mental, auditory, and even tactile, all so closely bound together that they are inseparable. Art is successful to the degree that it communicates this unique experience, to the degree in which it triggers in the spectator a similar response.

In the light of this theory of art, such terms as Renaissance, Baroque, and Mannerism can be seen as signifying certain emotional predispositions, a mood common to an age which results in similar artistic experiences. Although usually not written out explicitly, these basic attitudes are reflected in the way each artist experiences life. Style, because it is the language of art, is the way in which these attitudes are expressed. Historians therefore have grouped works of art around these categories according to style, and so it is to style that we must first turn our attention.

Because the subject matter of this essay is so varied, advice necessarily played a very large part in guiding my work from its inception to the final draft. My greatest debt is to Joseph T. Curtiss, my adviser, whose friendship, confidence, and scholarly vision sustained me throughout. I am also exceedingly grateful to Kurt Forster of the Yale University History of Art Department for his intimate knowledge of Mannerist art and his characteristically deep insight into the implications of that style. Irwin Gage, of the Yale School of Music, was invaluable for his generous help in the preparation of the section on Carlo Gesualdo. Further, I would like to thank Janet Knapp, Claude Palisca, Arthur Satz, and Charles Seymour for their freely given advice, and especially to thank Mrs. Robert J. Mittelstadt for the superb final typing of the manuscript under great pressure. Finally, I would like to thank my friends, both teachers and students, in the seminar of History, the Arts, and Letters at Yale for many ideas and criticisms.

Daniel B. Rowland

New Haven, Connecticut
September 1963

CONTENTS

1 TWO DEPOSITIONS:
AN INTRODUCTION TO MANNERISM
IN ART HISTORY

Deposition. (1503–1504).
Filippino Lippi & Pietro Perugino
Galleria Uffizi, Florence

Deposition. (1611–1614)
Peter Paul Rubens
Cathedral, Antwerp

Deposition. (1521)
Il Rosso Fiorentino
Pinacoteca, Volterra

Deposition. (1495)
Pietro Perugino
Palazzo Pitti, Florence.

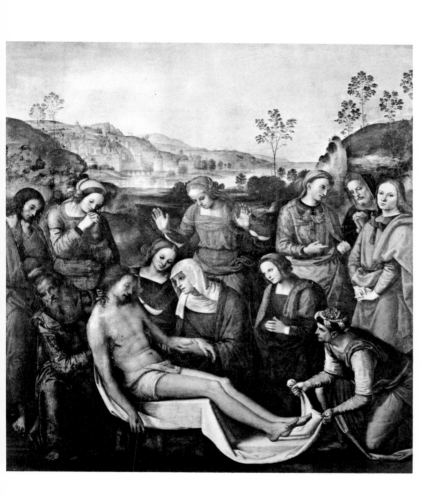

Deposition. (1507)
Raphael Sanzio
Galleria Borghese, Rome.

Deposition. (1601–1604)
Michelangelo Merisi da Caravaggio
Galleria Vaticana, Rome

Deposition. (1526–1528)
Jacopo da Pontormo
Santa Felicità, Florence.

F lorence in the 1520s was an unstable city. The political structure was alternately oppressive and chaotic, and the artistic leadership had already passed from Florence to the Rome of Julius II earlier in the century. Although one could hardly say that Florence was an artistic backwater at this time, the pulse of the city had slowed considerably with the exodus of such artists as Raphael and Michelangelo. Ideas from the north were coming into contact with the humanism and optimism of the Italian Renaissance. Martin Luther and Albrecht Dürer were both studied in Italy. Foreign armies were struggling for control of the peninsula. The decade was ushered in on the one hand by the death of Raphael in Rome and on the other by the burning of a Papal Bull by Martin Luther in Wittenberg. The next year Magellan returned from his trip around the world, and the old cosmography received a severe blow. The political ambitions of Italian city states were shattered by the entry of foreign invaders, and Florence herself fell after a siege in 1530. Rome was sacked in 1527. Several years before, the plague had swept Florence, bringing with it the great emotional strain common to all such visitations.

In the decade of the 1520s, two young artists, both pupils of the Renaissance master Andrea del Sarto, each painted a *Deposition*. These paintings are two of the most important monuments in Early Italian Mannerism. The first was done by Il Rosso Fiorentino in 1521 at Volterra, and reveals his first definitive break from the established style, after almost a decade of uneasy development. Rosso, as his name suggests, was an angry, violent man who murdered his servant in a fit of rage. By temperament, he was hostile to the more serene style of Andrea del Sarto, and had already stretched classical forms to their limit. In the *Deposition* at Volterra, Rosso made a final break with classicism, and achieved an entirely new form and new feeling, showing at once the essential elements of a new style and the effect of the artist's own fiery personality. In contrast to Rosso, Jacopo Pontormo, the artist of the second *Deposition*, was an almost pathological introvert, obsessed with the fear of death and resentful of the company of others. During the plague of

3

Florence, he fled for his life outside the city, and returned to paint his *Deposition* in the Capella Caponi at Santa Trinità between 1526 and 1528. Here again we can feel two elements at work, the strength of a new style and the extreme spirituality of the artist's personality.

It is curious that two of the central monuments of early Italian Mannerism should be depositions. Previous ages had attempted representations of this subject, but these had been neither particularly numerous nor successful. Many themes from the life of Christ had been explored in Christian art, but few artists had chosen to represent that particular moment when the lifeless body of Jesus was taken down from the cross, the darkest moment in Christianity, when the mortal Jesus, his agony finished, has been conquered by Death. There is no hint of the immortal Savior who, three days hence, would arise from the grave, the preordained and predestined victor. The crucifixion, a common enough theme in Christian art, was never just an image of despair, for there was always a struggle under way, a struggle in which Christ atoned for the sins of humanity. Christ crucified is at once an image of despair and triumph, and representations of this theme have always directed the emotions of the beholder toward the full significance of the scene within the drama of Christian salvation. The theme of the deposition does not lend itself to this treatment. The struggle is over, and the only evidence we have that Christ lived at all is the limp body in the arms of his disciples. From the point of view of the spectator, as in the minds of Christ's followers, this is indeed the darkest moment. The riddle of the life of Jesus is patently unsolved.

There were, however, several important depositions done in Florence in the period immediately preceding 1520. Pontormo and Rosso had before them a treatment of the same subject in a work started by Filippino Lippi and finished just after the beginning of the century by Perugino. This work shows the influence of the Late Gothic style, but is nevertheless best seen as a work of the Renaissance, containing as it does a rational space, an effort toward realistic treatment of figures, along with some idealization of form. The construction of Il Rosso's *Deposition* shows that in all likelihood he looked at this earlier work.

4

In order to grasp the relation of this painting, not only to the Renaissance, but also to the Baroque, we shall further examine another *Deposition*, this one by Peter Paul Rubens, now in the Cathedral at Antwerp.

The basic elements of the three *Depositions* are remarkably similar. All three show the dead Christ being lifted from the cross by figures on ladders set up against the cross, and in the left foreground all three artists have placed a group of grieving women. In addition, both Filippino Lippi and Rosso depict St. John and another figure in the right foreground. Rosso, however, makes a few important changes. Whereas in the earlier work Christ's body is the center of interest for the beholder as well as for the figures in the picture, Rosso has carefully diverted the eyes of his figures so that only one man is looking at Christ, and he is pointing at the wound in a demented fashion. (Everyone would have seen the pierced side by this time, and so the gesture itself is a meaningless repetition when seen in context. In the Lippi, this man is helping to carry Christ's body.) Aside from this one man, Rosso's figures stare into space in every conceivable direction, averting their eyes and the attention of the spectator away from the natural focus of attention, the body of Christ. Rosso has further introduced an old man overlooking the scene, his beard and cloak blowing in a wind that does not seem to affect the other figures; this man likewise stares into space, and seems to fulfill no useful function. Rubens, on the other hand, reduces the number of figures, and focuses all attention upon the corpse being lowered from the cross. The effect of the Rubens painting, with fewer figures and more concentrated psychological action, is to draw the attention of the viewer constantly back to Christ. This is true to a lesser extent with Filippino Lippi, the group of women in the left foreground taking one's eye temporarily away from the center of action, while the deposition remains the most important focal point. Rosso avoids any effect of focus, for by directing the attention of his figures out in many directions, he leads the eye of the viewer outward in a peculiar acentric pattern.

There are two essential problems which any artist dealing with this subject must meet. One is the structural opportunity offered by the cross itself, and this will be discussed later. The

5

other is the mechanical problem of getting the figure to the ground. The ladders were introduced partly to aid in this mechanical movement of a heavy mass. Filippino Lippi, though awkward in his treatment of the human anatomy, tries to achieve some sense of the weight of Jesus' body. The man on the left ladder does seem to be supporting a considerable weight. The two other figures show a remarkable sense of mechanical realism as they balance themselves against the weight of the body, one by curling his foot around his ladder, and the other by grasping the cloth tied around the top of the cross. Rubens is far more successful in his depiction of the great weight of the body, and in his treatment of anatomy. One can sense the downward pull on the drapery, the strain on Christ's left arm, the weight borne by the bent back of St. John as he supports the dead Christ. Rubens achieves a sense of the corporeal mass of Christ. Rosso, on the other hand, is less convincing in this matter than is Filippino Lippi. The man bearing most of the weight on the right holds the body only by one side, and his hand makes no attempt to grasp the chest of the cadaver. The figure holding the knees is in an even more precarious position. Indeed, he seems about to fall, for he has no counterbalance against the weight he bears, and anatomically, his right foot would be able to get a hold on the ladder only with greatest difficulty.

In Rosso the mechanical problem is not posed, for the reason that Christ's body is not as substantial as one might at first think. His right thigh has almost entirely dissolved, so that one can see the outline of the cross behind it, while his left foot and ankle seem to be following in its dissolution. There is little mechanical problem in moving an almost weightless body.

Although Pontormo's *Deposition* makes this point more clearly, we should note in passing Rosso's elongation of the figures, especially that of Christ, relative to figural proportions in Rubens or Filippino Lippi. More noticeable, however, is Rosso's seeming inverse idealization of the human face. Renaissance art theory demanded the selection of the most beautiful elements from various bodies. As Alberti and Leonardo both point out, this is not to be a process involving only the imagination, but must be based firmly on the study of nature.[1] In the

1. Anthony Blunt, *Artistic Theory in Italy, 1450–1600* (London, Oxford University Press, 1956), pp. 17, 18, 30.

figure of Christ, the most perfect human being, Filippino Lippi presents us with an idealization. Christ's face is serene and beautiful. Rubens is more realistic; Jesus looks dead and not asleep. Rosso, however, paints the most hideous grin possible, which is more than realistic; it is an extension of the hideousness of the real, which forcefully drives home the idea that Christ is dead. A similar tendency, without any apparent purpose, can be observed in the bearded figure by Rosso as compared to that of either Filippino or Rubens.

Perhaps the most obvious area in which Rosso differs from both Lippi and Rubens is in the modeling of his figures and their clothing. Rosso, by extending Andrea del Sarto's technique of forming figures out of tiny rationally constructed planes, arrived at a completely different result, allowing the planes to grow too large and to dominate the figures.[2] The result of this process is an almost cubist treatment, so that figures consist not of real flesh, but of planes. The best example of this treatment is Mary Magdalen, who stretches across the bottom of the composition. The half of her body facing the viewer consists of only two planes, which meet at a sharp angle. There is no attempt here to depict the anatomy of a real person. Instead Rosso emphasizes the angles produced by his planar treatment. One effect of this modeling is that we are never sure what exists on the side of the figure away from us. The figures sometimes seem to end with the jagged outline of their clothing, and a convincing three-dimensional effect is seldom achieved. This is especially true of the group of women in the left foreground. As the Magdalen's arm reaches between the first two women, one gets the impression of three planes on top of one another, with very little extension in depth, of paper cut-outs pasted against a background. Rosso thus takes an essentially Renaissance technique and, pushing it to its extreme limits, sacrifices the purpose.

2. "En fait la méthode d'Andrea del Sarto qui avec le clair-obscur, travaille la forme comme à la gradine dans un taillage à facettes progressif et rationnel des plans, est maintenant amenée par Rosso à une sorte de violence cubiste, à une obsession d'angles, d'arêtes, d'éclatement en copeaux, qui réduisent les figures à des abréviations essentielles, à des apparences cristallines déshumanisées, revêtues cependant de couleurs joyeuses et aigres, reflets éclantants de rubis, de topazes, d'émeraudes, sous un ciel lustré et pesant comme un cauchemar d'ardoise bleue." Giuliano Briganti, *Le Maniérisme Italien* (Leipzig, VEB Edition, 1962), p. 26.

for which this technique was evolved, that is, the convincing representation of three-dimensional figures having real weight. His style appears rough and crude as a result.

This exaggerated modeling technique is best seen in the treatment of clothing. The drapery surrounding the figures bears little resemblance to real costumes of a particular period, nor is it related to the anatomy of the human figure. The clothing of the man pointing at Christ's wound, for example, has no existence of its own, but seems to melt in with the hair or arm of its wearer. The clothing is often distorted for expressive purposes. The figure of St. John, on the far right, gains much of its impact from the jagged, nervous effect of the angles of the clothing, and from the sudden contrast between the sharp highlights and the darker areas. The rhythm created by the drapery is the dominant element in the figure, and is a powerful agent for the expression of the sharp grief the disciples must have felt at the time. However, this emphasis upon powerful and complex linear surface patterns, along with the unrealistic modeling, destroys a convincing effect of plasticity.[3]

Another reason for the feeling of two-dimensionality in the figures is the narrow space in which they exist as compared to the space created by Filippino Lippi in which his figures move freely. The figures in a deposition, by necessity, are mainly on one plane, that of the cross. The cross provides a vertical frame so that figures can fill the whole picture, and still exist logically at one distance from the viewer. Filippino Lippi counteracts this inherent tendency toward frontality in the subject by placing a fully developed landscape in the background, so that the front plane is related to a real space. Rosso, however, abstracts this landscape to a series of jagged outlines which are consistent with the angularity of the rest of the work, but bear no apparent relation to the space in the foreground. The tiny figures on the far right are in an abstract world separated by an indefinite amount of space from the scene of the deposition. Moreover, St. John, although seemingly on the same plane as the other figures, is drawn to a different scale, and looms too large in his grief. Rosso's space, then, is abstract and fragmented; there is no con-

3. Sydney Freedberg finds the same to be true of Parmigianino's early work. *Parmigianino*, p. 13.

sistent attempt to represent real space, but instead this element is used arbitrarily for expressive purposes.

The cross is also a very abstracted form. Rubens shows us the cross as it probably existed, two bits of wood rudely fastened together. Filippino Lippi idealizes this form somewhat, but Rosso presents us with an entirely abstract form, with no traces of its construction visible, seemingly hewn from one single piece of wood. Moreover, Rosso's cross is geometrical in its regularity. It has ceased to be the real cross on Calvary and has become a structural abstraction. Indeed, Rosso's painting can be considered as an abstraction of his probable model, Filippino's *Deposition.* Il Rosso's figures are not real figures, nor do they exist in a real space or even at a real time. It is neither day nor night, morning nor evening in Rosso's work. There is no visible atmosphere; instead we sense only the coldness of a vacuum. These figures inhabit an abstract world very different from the sensual world of experience. Peter Paul Rubens represents precisely the opposite tendency. His figures are real, particularized, and heavy; his space is convincing, and the time is shown by the lighting. He makes us feel the flesh, see the atmosphere of the scene. Rubens' world is the world of our sense experiences, and one of the purposes of his painting seems to have been to relate the events of the deposition to our concrete world of the here and now.

It has been mentioned before that one of the problems common to all three of these artists was the mechanical one of lowering the body to the ground. The second is the compositional problem posed by the existence of such a rigid and regular form as the cross. Filippino uses this form to dominate his composition. His figures are distinctly smaller than Rosso's in relation to the cross and are governed primarily by the vertical shank. The primary emphasis is upon the vertical, and Christ as well as the rest of the figures lies parallel to this general movement. Rosso, however, partly because of the increased size of his figures, sets up rhythms conflicting with the stable vertical-horizontal of the cross. He introduces a third ladder at an angle to the shank of the cross, and then creates, in the limbs and clothing of the figures at the top of the cross, a complex set of counter-rhythms on this diagonal line and on another line

9

at right angles to it. Thus working against the vertical-horizontal right angle is this second set of angles at 30 degrees or so to the vertical. Also, into this already complex pattern is introduced yet another angle, made by the arm pointing at Christ's wound, and emphasized by its solitary position in the middle of an empty space. The group at the foot of the cross consists of two groups of verticals joined by the vermilion zigzag line of Mary Magdalen. Rosso's compositional pattern, then, is complex and full of potential disturbance. Its comprehension demands a refined sensitivity to linear patterns not required in the reading of simple regular shapes. Yet this pattern is a very strong element in which every line takes part. This is no haphazard order, but one very carefully worked out to hold the composition together.

Rubens handles the cross in a completely different way. His composition, emphasized by his use of chiaroscuro, centers all the action upon a dramatic diagonal line running from upper right to lower left. In a fashion typically Baroque, all other movements are subordinated to this one diagonal, and the cross therefore is almost completely obliterated either by other things, or by the chiaroscuro. Rubens thus gains a strong sense of focus upon this one overpowering diagonal, and upon the body which lies at its center. There is a strong directional pull in the composition, for all the lines in the picture bring the eye back to this point of focus.

There is no similar focus anywhere in the Rosso, except perhaps on the two negative spaces enclosed by the network of bodies. Psychologically, such a focus is difficult to understand, because the lower empty area centers around Christ's feet, while the upper one, smaller and off-center, emphasizes the meaningless action of pointing at Christ's wound. Around these two clearly defined empty spaces swirl the complex and nervous rhythms of bodies, ladders, and clothing falling in angular folds. The eye is led into the picture by the strongly lighted bottom corner of St. John's cloak, and follows the jagged lines of his clothing to the ladder, which in turn leads up into the complex of right angles at the top of the picture. Finally, one's eye escapes to the group of women, and from them, via the angles of Mary Magdalen's dress, back to the starting place.

10

All this complex motion is too much for the eye to grasp, and, stepping back to get an overall view of the work, one cannot easily understand its structure. The eye is constantly drawn away from the central negative spaces to the outside, and is kept there by the complex and rough rhythmic patterns. Exactly contrary to the Rubens, this work focuses outward compositionally as well as psychologically, or better has no focus but a strong acentric centrifugal tendency. There is no unambiguous directional pull.

Rosso's *Deposition,* then, is exceedingly complex. The unity that might have been gained by a rational spatial container or by a strongly focused composition has been neglected in favor of an intricately interwoven and "unreadable" pattern not easily grasped by the eye. The jagged lines and angles prevent any sense of flow from one part to another. Instead the picture seems fragmented, and the compartmented space adds to this impression of fragmentation. Rosso has given us a picture of an abstract world, sharply divided from the here and now by the front plane of the picture, a private world unrelated to the real, where bodies consist of planes and have little solidity, where there is no sense of time or real space. The characters themselves become abstractions of demented grief. (See the woman on the far left, or St. John, for example.) Negative spaces emphasize the importance of unimportant elements. The style is purposely rough and jagged. All these elements suggest a form of art deliberately cut off from the easily understandable, a world of uncertainty and instability, where the equilibrium is upset by counter forces. The exact meaning of the painting remains unclear. Nevertheless, it succeeds brilliantly (and perhaps far better than the other two in terms of twentieth-century interpretation) in portraying the hopeless grief and the sense of meaninglessness which must have characterized the real deposition.

Rosso completed his painting in 1521, and left two years later for Rome. Jacopo Pontormo, his fellow experimenter in the anticlassical style, remained in Florence, save for the time he was driven out by the plague. Returning after the nightmare of the epidemic was over, Pontormo began work on his *Deposition* in 1526, and finished it in 1528. He abandoned Rosso's cross, and presents us with Christ already off the cross being carried by two men and surrounded by eight other figures. The absence of the cross, which Rosso had used as a structure to allow all his figures to remain logically close to the front plane of the picture, made it necessary for Pontormo to pile up his figures, crowding them on top of one another. In thus abandoning the representation of the cross itself, Pontormo moved into a slightly different tradition, and must have used different paintings as prototypes.

Pietro Perugino, who finished the Filippino Lippi *Deposition* we have just been examining, also painted another *Deposition* dated 1495, this time entirely his own, which is now in the Pitti Palace in Florence. In this *Deposition* Perugino, like Pontormo, omits the cross and shows us the dead Christ surrounded by his followers. Unlike Pontormo, however, he does not fill the entire picture surface with figures, but places his figures in a clearly defined landscape and in a rational space. It is very probable that Pontormo saw this early work, and used it as one of his models. Perugino's pupil, Raphael, also painted a similar *Deposition,* and the reaction of these two different painters to the same theme provides us with some insights into the difference between a Renaissance and a Mannerist sensibility. The same theme, with some variation, was taken up by Caravaggio between 1601 and 1604,[4] and his solution indicates many of the Baroque tendencies involved in all of this artist's work.

The scenes presented to us by both Perugino and by Raphael are static. Raphael has abolished the one dramatic movement in Perugino's *Deposition,* the hands of the woman behind the body thrown up in surprise. Although the landscape is realistic, as is the atmosphere, the dramatic action of the figures has been stopped. Neither Raphael nor Perugino represents a specific moment in time, but rather a generalized moment sometime before the entombment and after the actual deposition. Pontormo abstracts this further, separating his scene from any reference to physical reality. Pontormo's figures are in a timeless frozen world completely foreign to the full daylight and the pleasant landscapes of Perugino and Raphael. There is no attempt made

4. Dates given by Roberto Longhi, *Il Caravaggio* (Milan, Aldo Martello, 1951), note for plate xxix.

in either the Pontormo or the Rosso to bring their representations into a common frame of reference with the experience of the viewer by the inclusion of details from the real world.

The space in Pontormo's *Deposition* displays the same characteristics as the space in Rosso's work, but the effect is more obvious because of the absence of the cross. The ample space of the two Renaissance works is transformed into a narrow slice of space, the back plane of which is indicated by the woman at the very top of the picture. The figures cannot logically fit into this space; there is, for example, no room for the body of the head seen directly above Christ's head. Although there is little of the two-dimensional cut-out effect which we observed in Rosso's work, the compression of space is greater. Yet in spite of this compression, no part of the picture projects into the space beyond the front plane of the picture. The effect of this crowding into a narrow space is like that of a lot of children anxiously peering into a candy-store window. The storekeeper inside is made much more aware of the presence of the glass by the fact that the children are crowding against it. In the same way, the spectator is made to sense the front plane of the picture, the very definite barrier that separates Pontormo's world from his own. Caravaggio, on the other hand, brings the spectator visually into his *Deposition* by showing the stone on which the figures stand as projecting beyond the surface of the canvas into the space of the viewer. This stone forms a visual bridge between the two worlds which is paralleled psychologically by the gaze of the man in brown out at the spectator.

The two High Renaissance artists idealized the real world, but still remained very much in touch with it, for their ideal was based on nature. They thus achieved a balance between abstraction and reality. Caravaggio tended to move in the opposite direction, to neglect abstraction in order to bring his creation in touch with the real world. He represents an actual moment, the specific act of lowering Christ's body into the Sepulchre, in a specific place. The dramatic gesture abolished by Raphael is replaced. Caravaggio is the only one of the four artists who presents us with a convincing dramatic scene where something is actually going on. Perugino's scene is a static tableau with Christ's body at rest. In the Raphael, two figures have picked up the body, but they are not moving in any particular direction, and the psychological action of the other figures is unrelated to any action aside from the generalized expression of sorrow. The elements are taken from the natural world, but there is no dramatic situation. In Caravaggio's *Deposition,* however, there is definite action, and the attention of all the figures save one is focused upon it. Caravaggio's figures behave as one would expect them to. His drama is convincing.[5] Only the girl in the back acts in a way unexplained by the obvious facts of the dramatic situation, and her gesture may be interpreted as a rhetorical one of violent grief.

Pontormo's picture by contrast is completely undramatic. The figures all look away from what should be the center of attention—Christ's body. There is little sense of motion or effort in the figures carrying the body; they are not moving in any direction, nor are they in any position capable of movement, as Raphael's men are. There is no declamation in the distracted gestures of Pontormo's figures, as there is in the upraised arms of Caravaggio's girl. Seen within the context of the work of Raphael and Caravaggio, Pontormo's figures lack at once the static firmness of one and the dramatic action of the other.

Including the body of Christ, there are twelve figures in Perugino's *Deposition.* Raphael has cut the number to ten, divided down the center of the picture into two balanced groups of five each. Caravaggio has condensed the number to six, and these six he has arranged in a very tight form resembling a right triangle. There is no division into groups, and the small number of people and the compact design Caravaggio has formed produce a composition more focused than that of the Renaissance works. The focus is upon the body of Christ, which is emphasized by its whiteness, and placed dramatically at an angle to the picture plane. To Christ's body radiate almost all the lines of the composition, as they did in the Rubens. The effect, however, is even greater, because these very lines have been foreshortened, due to the position of the spectator below the group.

5. Walter Friedlaender makes this point of the drama in Caravaggio more extensively. *Caravaggio Studies* (Princeton, Princeton University Press, 1955).

Pontormo moves against this tendency to lessen the number of figures, and chooses the uneven number of eleven, which is not broken into any distinct groups. With no discernible pattern to order them, these figures swim incomprehensibly in front of the eye. If there were only three figures, or even five, the eye could impose its own order; it could "read" or understand the relation between them. The eleven figures Pontormo presents us with are too numerous for this to occur, however, and we are bewildered. There is a total lack of any dominant element for our eye to center on, for Christ's body, which was the focus for Caravaggio, is off-center, and merely a part of the centrifugal swirl of bodies. Like Rosso's *Deposition,* Pontormo's work is acentric in composition, and we find a similar use of negative space in the strange hole in the center filled only by arms.

In this space, Pontormo has taken what was an extremely minor theme in Perugino and Raphael, a woman holding the hand of Christ, and expanded it in an entirely illogical way. Two arms, seemingly coming out of nowhere, are holding Christ's arm and hand. They appear to belong to the head which mysteriously exists in the space directly above Christ's head, but there is no indication of, or space for, the rest of the body. Moreover, the head is distinctly looking away from what the hands are doing.

Around this hole or negative space, the tortured bodies move in an oval pattern. The rhythm created by the billowy drapery is the opposite of that found in Rosso's sharp angular composition, but the effect is the same. The eye can never come to rest on anything, but is kept constantly traveling around and around the composition following the curving lines of drapery until a sense of nausea is produced. Just as one feels nauseous at sea when motion is constant and there is no firm place to rest, so Pontormo produces a kind of visual nausea.[6] The eye can grasp no pattern, so it travels endlessly over the billowy surface rhythms of drapery.

6. "It is impossible to sing three such pieces one after another (madrigals by Carlo Gesualdo, book VI) without being seized by a sort of nausea or musical sea-sickness, for the dose is too strong, and the unsteadiness too prolonged." Alfred Einstein, *The Italian Madrigal* (Princeton, Princeton University Press, 1949), *3,* 715.

15

Nevertheless, one must not suppose that the painting lacks a pattern. On the contrary, Pontormo, like Rosso, has created a complex and tightly knit pattern which involves every shape in the entire work. Although the composition is acentric, nothing could be taken out without upsetting this delicate network. The seemingly irrelevant cloud, for example, has a multiple reference to the shapes around it, to the woman leaning over in the upper left and to the youth with outstretched hands in the top right.[7] Across the center of the picture is a distinct V shape, the point of which is the head of the figure holding Christ's shoulders, and the arms of which are indicated by the two heads immediately to the right of this point. But each of the shapes which make up this V also participate in one or more other patterns. The result is a very complex network which has no central focal point, but which nevertheless succeeds in keeping each part of the work in its exact place. To move anything would be to destroy this pervasive but delicate network.

Even more than the ceaseless motion, Pontormo's use of color contributes to the feeling of nausea. The color schemes of both Raphael and Caravaggio are at once moderately realistic and harmonious. Rosso's colors were often frankly dissonant, but Pontormo carries this tendency to an extreme. The coloring of his figures has no reference in reality. The figure in the center foreground, for example, has an orchid-colored body and arm. Bright reds, pale pinks, light yellows, and light grey-blues, yellowish and off-shade greens all conflict in the drapery of the figures. Pink areas cast orange shadows. Much of the emotional impact of the picture is conveyed by this juxtaposition of opposed colors; it is plain that Pontormo purposely created this strangely exotic color scheme, and that through the juxtaposition of violently opposed colors, he expressed the profound sense of grief implicit in the theme of the deposition.

The most striking emotion, however, is expressed by the figures themselves. Their haunted and demented images remain imprinted on the memory, so expressive are they of an unknowable grief. A comparison of the figural treatment of Pontormo with that of Raphael and Caravaggio will help to

7. This feature was pointed out by Kurt Forster of the Yale University History of Art Department, April 1963.

16

reveal how Pontormo achieves this effect, and will cast light on his view of man.

The figural treatment of the three artists differs most obviously over the problem of realism. As we have repeatedly seen, Caravaggio follows nature, Raphael idealizes nature, and Pontormo almost abandons nature in pursuit of his own private ideal. The treatment of the feet of the figure holding Christ's legs illustrates this generalization. Pontormo's figures are greatly elongated compared with the Renaissance ideal, but they are elegant in their own refined sense. The heads of the figures, for example, are all almost perfect ovals, geometric but not realistic. Pontormo pays little attention to the muscular system that Caravaggio is so careful to show, but instead distorts his bodies to gain elegance or rhythmical effect. The waist of the man nearest the viewer in the foreground is abnormally high; anatomically it is impossible to bend one's body from a point so high up on the torso, while keeping the bottom part of the trunk straight. There is no skeletal structure indicated for these figures. The treatment by Pontormo of Christ's body reveals a similar disregard for human anatomy.

Again like Rosso, but again more clearly, Pontormo uses the clothing of his figures in a purely arbitrary way. The costumes, both in form and color, are completely divorced from reality. Cloth fades imperceptibly into flesh, and the folds of the drapery billow up in contradiction to the laws of gravity. At the same time, their filmy transparency helps to dissolve any sense of solid form that the figures underneath may have had. As in Rosso, the drapery surrounding the figures is used for purely decorative and expressive purposes, and as a set of surfaces to contain the colors which Pontormo wanted to use.

All we can see, then, of Pontormo's figures is their surface, for there is no indication of the body underneath the skin. Sydney Freedberg observed the same tendency in the work of Parmigianino, a Mannerist artist contemporary to Pontormo, and came to the following conclusion, which applies in my opinion to Pontormo as well:

> Parmigianino's figures are an assembly of surfaces; nothing is contained within these surfaces, and their modeling

17

is the affirmation not of a solid, but only of a hollow form.[8]

This statement also reminds us of Rosso's Mary Magdalen. In contrast to the High Renaissance sense of physical mass contained within the surface, continues Freedberg, Parmigianino's surface is

> . . . in essence no more than a continuous boundary between the hollowness of the inner body and the surrounding space.[9]

With this view of the human figure, the problem of weight and mass did not exist for Pontormo the way that it did for Caravaggio and Raphael. That the figures carrying Christ should be balanced on their toes is not surprising if neither their bodies nor Christ's body has any weight. In fact, far more clearly than in Rosso, the forms seem to float in a kind of neutral world unaffected by the ordinary law of gravity. In this world there is no mass, no movement, no physical energy. Pontormo's world is one of an uneasy neutrality governed by complex surface patterns but not by any easily grasped laws.

Pontormo's figures are, then, expressive abstractions. He has rejected the Renaissance image of the self-sufficient man acting in a rational environment which he can understand. The environment has almost ceased to exist, and all that is visible is a few fragments which fail to fit together in any coherent pattern. In this world the Renaissance belief in the beauty and vigor of the human body is destroyed, for if Pontormo's figures are beautiful in a refined way, because of their perfectly oval faces or their other elegant forms, they are certainly not vigorous in a world where action is impossible. Because there is no apparent reason for their weird circle dance, the relationship between these figures is ill-defined psychologically as well as spatially. Rather they seem controlled by unknown forces, forces unaccounted for by the Renaissance world view, and not fully understandable by anyone.

Whereas the other painters we have been examining chose to express themselves in terms of a world governed by numerous

8. Freedberg, *Parmigianino*, p. 14.
9. Ibid.

systems, it is peculiar to Pontormo and Rosso that they avoided creating any patterns save that of a complex and indefinite surface linear rhythm. Indeed their emotion is expressed by the breaking of laws just as the other artists expressed themselves through these laws. Raphael expressed his emotion in a rational space; Rosso's grief found expression only in breaking the space. Rubens and Caravaggio, and to a lesser extent Perugino and Raphael, depicted scenes in which the emotions were conveyed by a logical-psychological framework within the picture. Rosso and Pontormo broke this framework, and achieved their expression in the very act of breaking it. A consistent drama would have been for them less effective, because they felt that the highest reality is not governed by systems or common frames of reference. Thus these painters broke almost every formal system they could find, leaving only a complex and finally incomprehensible pattern. They fragmented space, so that the spatial frame of reference was gone; they abstracted time, so that in their two *Depositions* there is no time; they altered and abstracted the human form so that there is no human frame of reference; their figures seem to be under mysterious supernatural direction; they attacked the validity of the third dimension, and almost did away with the concept of plastic mass that gives two-dimensional patterns on a flat surface any meaning or relevance to the three-dimensional world we inhabit; they broke down any obvious system of color harmony in their violent juxtaposition of discordant colors. Expression was for the first time thought of in terms outside the usual frames of reference. The disrupting forces represented, instead of operating within these accepted patterns, break through them, and in so doing reveal their strength.

Two corollaries follow from this idea. One is that both paintings we have been studying are exceedingly difficult to understand. Our understanding works through just those frames of reference which Pontormo and Rosso purposely broke. Caravaggio's work, being dramatic, is comprehended through a psychological framework based on common experience. In short, he speaks in terms we can understand. Pontormo and Rosso break this frame of reference to express themselves, but in so doing become less immediately understandable. They cannot

19

communicate via a rational framework and break that framework at the same time. Their art is therefore relatively inaccessible, their world seemingly separated from the common-sense world of the here and now.

The other corollary is that the art of a Pontormo or a Rosso is in many senses a self-conscious, derivative, backward-looking art. It could not exist without rules to break, without a set of frameworks to smash. The artist must be conscious of both the rules and the fact that he is breaking them. The style of these two artists could not have existed without the High Renaissance, and cannot be considered except in relation to this style.

The unity of Renaissance painting gained by numerous systems of harmony and proportion is broken into pieces, and these pieces, unchangeable in themselves, like past events in the memory, are then reassembled so that all the systems are out of joint. The skill of these artists lies in the fact that their art is unified by a beautifully intricate surface pattern. The floating pieces remaining from the memory of the Renaissance are not just thrown together, but are placed in patterns so skillful and delicate that any movement, even any noise, would cause the whole to crumble. Much later, when the systems of the Renaissance had faded from the mind, critics could not see what was being broken, and Mannerist art naturally struck them as manneristic, as a needless repetition of intricate formal patterns. As soon as a memory of and a yearning for the Renaissance had ceased to exist, then Mannerist art was impossible and meaningless.

2 CARLO GESUALDO:
MANNERISM IN THE MADRIGAL

Don Carlo Gesualdo, Prince of Venosa, composed the madrigal *Io parto* approximately eighty years after Il Rosso Fiorentino finished his *Deposition*. Far from being a seminal figure, as were the first generation Mannerist painters, Gesualdo came at the end of a progression of madrigal composers, and after he had written there was little room for further development. By 1611, when he first published his fifth and sixth books of madrigals, Mannerism, never very fully developed, was at best a minor current in musical thought. The corresponding period in the visual arts can boast few artists of stature, but in music Gesualdo stands as one of the most skillful as well as one of the most extreme composers in what one may call the Mannerist style of composition. In fact, it is perfectly possible that Gesualdo was the only fully developed Mannerist, and this fact would help to explain why his art could occur so late and yet escape the dry formality which befell late Mannerist painters. Moreover, the Renaissance style of composition lasted in sacred music at least until the close of the seventeenth century, and this delay and extension of the musical Renaissance would have left Gesualdo very much in touch with the Renaissance currents that a Mannerist artist must feel directly if his art is to have force. Whatever the cause, his music shows the same centrifugal qualities which we have seen in Rosso and Pontormo. Gesualdo seems equally anxious to break through the stylistic systems of his day; like them he never constructed a new system, but built his madrigals out of the fragments of what he had destroyed, fragments put together with consummate skill into a delicate structure.

In moving from the realm of painting to that of music we must note a few distinctions inherent in the very nature of the latter art form, for we cannot expect from music the kind of explicit statement which poetry, and painting to a lesser extent, can give us. We have seen how Pontormo's view of man was expressed in his treatment of the human figure and his depiction of the environment in which his figures exist. Music by itself lacks the ability to communicate such philosophic concepts. Tones arranged in patterns cannot specifically depict

23

either man or his environment. Without words, music is the most purely formal of any of the arts; by nature it is abstract, and by nature, therefore, style is of great importance. Fortunately, Gesualdo wrote music with words, and his text provides us with a useful entrance to the music. Gesualdo did not write his own texts, however, and to penetrate the meaning of his work at all deeply, we must analyze the more formal aspects of his music. As in the visual arts, we shall constantly examine Gesualdo, not as an isolated figure, but in relation to composers of the Renaissance and the Baroque, for Gesualdo, like Rosso and Pontormo, was faced with the inheritance of a classic art form governed by rules of proportion and order, and only by examining his relation to this tradition and to the new developments of the Baroque may we accurately assess his style.

Even a casual glance at music theorists of the sixteenth century will reveal a striking similarity between their views of the *ars perfecta* of Netherlandish polyphony and the views of Renaissance art theorists on the art of the High Renaissance. Both art and music theorists of the period looked back to antiquity as the last great flowering of artistic talent before their own time. Both disciplines subscribed to the Renaissance theory that the Middle Ages were a period of darkness and that only their present age approached the achievements of the ancients. Music was thus included in the general cultural movement known as the Renaissance. Musicians, as well as men of letters, painters, sculptors, and architects, began examining the past and gained a new sense of their own perfection, a sense of their superiority to the unskilled work of the previous age. This confidence was caused by new technical achievements in both art and music, which enabled both composer and artist of the early sixteenth century to consider their work as clearly superior technically to that of previous centuries. These men saw themselves at the culmination of a long historical development. The Netherlandish polyphony of Josquin, as well as the art of Raphael, was looked upon as a perfect art that could not be surpassed.

This attitude toward the musical achievement of the Renaissance had already manifested itself by 1475 in the writings of Johannes Tinctoris, himself a Netherlander. In the preface of his significantly titled *Proportionale Musices* he writes:

24

At this time, consequently, the possibilities of our new music have been so marvellously increased that there appears to be a new art, if I may so call it, whose fount and origin is held to be among the English, of whom Dunstable stood forth as chief. Contemporary with him in France were Dufay and Binchoys, to whom directly succeeded the moderns, Ockeghem, Busnoys, Regis, and Caron, who are the most excellent of all the composers I have ever heard.[1]

Moreover, in the dedicatory prefaces to both the *Proportionale* and the *Liber de arte contrapuncti* (1477), Tinctoris alludes frequently and at great length to the writers of antiquity, and in so doing reveals another facet of his affinity to Renaissance thought. By 1547 and the *Dodecachordon* of Heinrich Glarean, Josquin des Prés has become the model, the ultimate step in the historical development Tinctoris saw as beginning with Dunstable.

Josquin, however, was never captivated by the madrigal, although he did write many secular *chansons*. The madrigal is a peculiarly Italian form with a traditionally strong emphasis upon the text. The composers of Josquin's generation declined to contribute to the madrigal, which they felt was a local artless form not worthy of their talents.[2] The French *chanson* was more suited to their tastes, and left them free from formal restrictions which might spoil the perfection of the *ars perfecta*. The madrigal was taken up, however, by three composers of the succeeding generation of Netherlanders, or *Oltremontani* as the Italians called them. Adrian Willaert, Jacob Arcadelt, and Cipriano da Rore all adapted the native Italian madrigal to their own polyphonic style. Thus at the beginning the madrigal was another outlet for the universally acclaimed new style. However, as these men continued to write, and as other composers, both Italian and foreign, joined them, the madrigal began to develop a style of its own, different in several ways from the style of the *ars perfecta*. It is beyond the scope of this essay to deal with this later madrigal school as a whole. That the entire Italian madrigal school can be considered Mannerist is

1. Oliver Strunk, *Source Readings in Music History* (New York, Norton, 1950), p. 195.
2. Leo Schrade, *Monteverdi, Creator of Modern Music* (New York, Norton, 1950), pp. 56–58.

very doubtful, but our concern lies only with one of the last of the madrigalists, Carlo Gesualdo.

In searching for a Renaissance work to compare with Gesualdo's *Io parto*, we must go back to the first Netherlandish madrigalists, for they preserve most closely the style of the *ars perfecta* within the form of the madrigal. Later composers changed the style, and the madrigal under their hands lost some of its classical qualities. In the opinion of Vincenzo Galilei, father of the astronomer and scientist Galileo Galilei, Cipriano da Rore was one of the greatest of these composers:

> And all the best practical musicians agree in saying and believing that between that time [c. 1430] and this [1581], music has reached the highest perfection that man can imagine, indeed that since the death of Cipriano Rore, a musician truly unique in this matter of counterpoint, *it has rather declined than advanced*.[3]

Vincenzo was a member of the Florentine *camerata* which produced the first opera and which was thus in the forefront of the new Baroque style in music—accompanied monody. There is an interesting parallel here between Galilei's view of the art of the preceding century, and that expressed by such early Baroque artists as Annibale Carracci. Both painter and composer traced the decline in their art from the death of the Renaissance masters.

From Cipriano's work I have chosen *Quando lieta sperai* as an example of the classical Renaissance madrigal. The text, as in most madrigals, deals with disappointed love. The logical choice for an early Baroque madrigalist falls upon Claudio Monteverdi, the key figure in the development of the new style. Monteverdi's fourth book of madrigals was the last which did not demand some form of instrumental accompaniment, and from this book, we may take *Si ch'io vorrei morire* as a typical example of the most fully developed Baroque madrigal that had not yet abandoned the traditional five-voice texture.

Carlo Gesualdo's personality is as famous as his music. His tumultuous life, and especially the murder of his wife, her lover, and his second son (who, suspiciously, resembled the lover),

3. Strunk, pp. 305–06 (italics are mine).

26

have made Don Carlo a fascinating figure aside from his music, but the details of this life have been treated adequately elsewhere.[4] It is sufficient here to mention that the Prince shared personality traits with both Pontormo and Rosso. Like Rosso, he had a violent temper and was a murderer. Like Pontormo, he was obsessed by the fear of death, as is shown by his extraordinary emphasis upon the word *morte* whenever it appears in his texts. *Io parto* appears in Book VI of Gesualdo's madrigals, published in 1611, two years before his death. Though roughly contemporary with Monteverdi's Book IV, this madrigal shows at once that these two composers represent different musical schools. As the history of music has shown, Monteverdi's style swelled to dominate the entire musical world, whereas of Gesualdo's style very little further was heard. Gesualdo's music, with its tendency toward acentricity and its refusal to be governed by any system, would have been understandable by a few at best. The time was past, however, for in the excitement over the new, easily understood Baroque style, Gesualdo's music was gradually forgotten.

Perhaps the best way to begin a discussion of these madrigals is with a consideration of the text. Each text was vitally important as the subject matter, the very center of the madrigal, and as such greatly influenced the style of the work. The following are the texts chosen by the three various composers with translations gleaned from various sources.[5] Their individual choices are significant as indicating their individual taste in poetry.

4. Philip Heseltine and Cecil Grey, *Carlo Gesualdo, Prince of Venosa, Musician and Murderer* (London, Curwen and Sons, 1926). Aldous Huxley, *Tomorrow and Tomorrow and Tomorrow and Other Essays* (New York, Harper, 1956).

5. The translations of *Io parto* and *Si ch'io vorrei morire* are based upon translations found on record covers. The Gesualdo text was translated by Robert Craft for his Columbia recording (ML5234) and the Monteverdi text by Chester Kallman for Columbia recording (ML5159) by the Pro Musica Antiqua. Cipriano's text was translated by the author with the help of Victor Brombert of the Yale French Department and John Frissora of the Yale Italian Department.

In no case have I tried to recreate the original poetry in English. My purpose has been to give the reader a line-by-line translation which will enable him, with some imagination, to grasp the meaning of the Italian words, and so to follow the musical treatment of these words in the madrigals.

27

Quando lieta sperai (music by Cipriano)
> Quando lieta sperai siderm'all' ombra
> Tra bei purpurei fior del nuov' Aprile
> E cantand'obliar mio stat'humile,
> Tenendo sol d'amor l'anim'ingombra,
> Ecco Euro, ecc' Aquilon che'l mond'adombra
> Di nivol'e di pioggi' entr'a l'ovile.
> Trista mi chiude, e'l mio sperar gentile
> Con rabbioso soffiar subito sgombra,
> Tal ch'io non spero che mi s'apra mai
> Più chiar'il ciel'o più tranquill'un giorno:
> Tanto di ben mi fur le stell'avare.
> Lagrime dunque e sempiterni guai,
> Statemi pur eternalmente intorno,
> Sin ch'el fin giunga alle mie pen'amare.

Translation
> When happy I hoped I would sit in
>   the shadows
> Among the beautiful purple flowers
>   of the new April
> And singing, forget my humble condition
> Alone, my soul laden with love,
> Here is the east wind, here is the north wind
>   which darkens the world
> With clouds and rain inside the sheepfold.
> Sad, I am enveloped, and my gentle hope
> With angry gusts is suddenly cast away,
> So that I do not hope will open to me
> The sky clear, or calm, at any time:
> The stars were tightfisted when they
>   distributed good to me,
> Tears, therefore, and eternal woe
> Encompass [imperative form] me always
> Until the end comes to my bitter pains.

Si ch'io vorrei morire (music by Monteverdi)
> Si ch'io vorrei morire hora ch'io bacio, amore,
> La bella bocca del mio amato core.

Ahi, car'e dolce lingua,
Datemi tant'humore
Che di dolcezz' in questo sen m'estingua;
Ahi, vita mia, a questo bianco seno,
Deh stringetemi fin ch'io venga meno.
Ahi bocca, ahi baci,
Ahi lingua torn' a dire
Si ch'io vorrei morire.

Translation

Now would I die as I kiss, love,
The lovely mouth of my heart's desire.
Ah, sweet tongue, dear tongue
Give me such humours
Drawn of that breast that I may be
    smothered with sweetness;
Ah, my love, unto that white breast
Crush me to compass my dwindling.
O mouth, O kisses,
O tongue, return to me that I may say
Now would I die.

Io parto (music by Gesualdo)

"Io parto" e non più dissi, che il dolore
Privò di vita il core.
Allor proruppe in pianto e disse Clori
Con interrotti omèi: "Dunque ai dolori
Io resto. Ah, non fia mai
Ch'io non languisca, in dolorosi lai."
Morto fui, vivo son, che i spirti spenti
Tornaro in vita a sì pietosi accenti.

Translation

"I take my leave," and no more could
    I say because grief
Deprived my heart of life.
For it broke forth in sighs, and said
With broken sobs, "Therefore may
    I never cease

To languish in dolorous lays."
I was dead, now I am alive because
     the dead spirits
Return to life at the sound of such
     piteous accents.

Gesualdo's text, as we shall see, has much in common with Donne's poetry. Both Cipriano and Monteverdi use texts that engage the sensual imagination of the reader. Cipriano refers to fields, flowers, cold wind, songs, and so forth, while Monteverdi is taken up with the sensual pleasures of love. The images in Cipriano are the conventional pastoral images, and thus trees and flowers signify happiness, and the cold north wind the despair of disappointed love. The imagery revolves around a landscape and changing weather, and the reader grasps the meaning of the poem by picturing the landscape, smelling the flowers, hearing the singing, and feeling the bite of Aquilon, the north wind. The poem puts an abstract idea, disappointed love, into tangible imagery. Monteverdi likewise delights in the sensual aspects of his love affair, in the kisses, in the tongue, in the breasts of his love.

Gesualdo, like Donne, makes almost no use of the senses in his text. There are no tears, there is no mouth, there is no delight in the evocation of the senses. Instead the poem revolves around a tightly knit paradox which never is finally resolved. Grief seems to have killed the spirit, but now an even more intense grief brings it to life. The heart, already dead, manages somehow to revive itself by its own piteous accents. There is no logical thread here to pull together the hyperboles and oxymora of which the poem is constructed. Even the syntactical structure is confused. The poem is not made accessible by references to the common-sense world of the senses, as are the other two poems. Its meaning is unclear, for it is more a string of words than a unit of thought.

The meaning of the texts used by both Cipriano and Monteverdi is much clearer. Both texts are longer than Gesualdo's and both try to say less within their limits. Monteverdi's text particularly makes use of frequent repetitions and dramatic exclamations which increase the emotional impact of the poem

30

but do not serve to further the argument. A line such as "Ahi bocca, Ahi baci" (l. 8) is included for the sound of the words, as well as for the images they evoke. "Bocca," "baci," and "lingua" occur separately in lines 1, 2, and 3, and when they are repeated rapidly one after the other at the end of the poem, a dramatic effect is achieved. The tension is released as the poem ends with the same words with which it began in a kind of poetic *da capo*. Gesualdo's text makes use of none of these devices. Where Monteverdi is dramatic and repetitive, Gesualdo is complex and epigrammatic.

In the musical treatment of his text, Gesualdo obscures rather than emphasizes whatever slight logical unity his text may have had. His basic treatment of text differs from that of both Monteverdi and Cipriano. Although Monteverdi is more concerned with his text than is Cipriano, both consider the words, not individually, but as they make up a line or a thought. Only if it is consistent with the general atmosphere of a given line or thought may a "madrigalism" be introduced on a given word. Cipriano's *Quando lieta sperai* reveals a consistency which dominates madrigalisms on separate words. The slow rising movement on the words "E cantan" (measure 10–15) gives the effect of singing, but at the same time this movement is consistent with the overall texture at that point. The same may be said for the treatment of "obliar" which immediately follows. Even the madrigalism on "subito sgombra" (measure 40) does not interrupt the flow of the madrigal. Indeed, part of the mastery of Cipriano is shown in his ability to combine madrigalisms in the separate parts into a unified, complex whole. Moreover, although the imitative polyphonic technique obscures the words as they are sung, Cipriano pays careful attention to line endings or important pauses in the thought of the text by marking them with cadences. In measures 33 and 34, there is a cadence on the word "ovile" indicating the end of the sentence. There is similarly a cadence on the word "avare" (measures 55–58). Cipriano's musical structure thus reinforces the structure of the text.

Like Caravaggio, Monteverdi is concerned with the dramatic implications of his art. Cipriano's music emphasized the sentence and line structure of the text and kept madrigalisms under control. Monteverdi's setting goes beyond this, for the virtual creator of opera was naturally far more concerned with his text than was Cipriano. In the latter the musical form dominated the text, but Monteverdi combined a new structure with his desire to bring out the dramatic implications of his text. The unified musical texture of Cipriano is gone, but the diverse sections of the piece are held together by the dramatic structure of the text. This is not the static art of Cipriano, for the sections work against each other, but always with the result that they bring out the meaning of the text more clearly. His treatment of "Ahi car'e dolce lingua" (measures 15–26), because it is a marked change from the chordal texture of the previous section, comes at a point in the text where a statement is succeeded by an impassioned cry. The contrast of textures brings this change into sharper relief. The effect of this new psychological and dramatic realism is increased by Monteverdi's adaptation of his music to the sound of actual speech, by his attempt to capture the "accents of passion" in his madrigal.

Like Monteverdi, Gesualdo abandoned the uninterrupted texture of the *ars perfecta*. *Io parto* is broken into numerous small sections, each followed by its own cadence, and most separated from the other sections by frequent rests for all voices. The flow of the thought, although never completely destroyed, is constantly interrupted by these overly frequent cadences. We can thus see the same tendency to fragment or interrupt the flow which we observed in Pontormo and Rosso.

Gesualdo seems at first, like Monteverdi, to be centering his musical structure around the dramatic structure of his text. He begins with a section of simultaneous declamation, as does Monteverdi, and succeeds this section with an imitative section on "che il dolore" which is consistent musically and dramatically with the first section. His treatment of the next line, however, would be completely foreign to Monteverdi. The sense of the text runs over from line 1 to line 2; "Che il dolore privò di vita il core" is one thought (grief deprived my heart of life). This thought fits perfectly into the argument of the text. Gesualdo breaks the thought into parts, however, and treats it not as a unit of sense but as a group of words. Thus "che il dolore" is treated chromatically with very slow movement; "privò" is simultaneously declaimed; and "di vita il core" is set to very rapid, cheerful imitation, with bright harmonies ending splendidly on a G major triad. By separating "privò" from "di vita," Gesualdo actually reverses the sense of the text. The madrigalism, which had been a decoration in Cipriano or Monteverdi, has become dominant, overpowering alike the meaning of the text and the unity of the texture,[6] interrupting the natural flow of the thought.

As an exponent of the classic polyphonic style, Cipriano was mainly concerned not with the text, but with maintaining the perfection of his form. We therefore must guard against placing too much emphasis on his treatment of text; in order fully to appreciate Cipriano's art, one must look to his counterpoint. The beauty of the style of the *Oltremontani* consisted in the combination of different melodies sung at the same time, each having an independent existence of its own, yet each contributing to a unified harmonious effect. Unity was achieved by the successive imitation of one voice by the others. An examination of Cipriano's separate parts reveals that he was indeed an accomplished master of this *ars perfecta*. Each line moves in a stepwise fashion, independent rhythmically and harmonically from the other parts. Each makes an acceptable melody by itself, rhythmically diverse and completely devoid of ugly jumps which would break the melodic flow. One cannot help admiring the refined melodic technique Cipriano shows in this madrigal. At the same time, he uses the device of imitation to unify the piece both vertically and horizontally. The musical phrases in the various parts overlap, so that by the time the tenor and bass have finished the phrase ending with "Aprile" in measure 10, for example, the cantus and altus have already begun their next phrase. Moreover, as each part answers the cantus' stepwise melody on "E cantan" (measures 10–15) with exactly the same melody and words, a vertical homogeneity is achieved. In contrast to earlier music, there is no fundamental distinction in the character of the various voices. They all sing the same type of

6. I do not mean to imply that all sudden contrasts are undramatic. Gesualdo's treatments of "Morto fui, vivo son" later in the madrigal is fully justified because it brings out a dramatic contrast contained in the text. In the case under discussion, however, this dramatic contrast is clearly not contained in the text.

independent but related melody, and yet together they form a unity both vertically and horizontally. There is no point in the entire piece where all the voices rest at once, and the result is a smooth, uninterrupted texture. A further effect of symmetry is achieved by having the imitating voices enter at regular rhythmic intervals, as can be seen again in measures 10–15. In Cipriano's hands, then, the Renaissance polyphonic technique serves as a very powerful unifying system, a system to which all other considerations are subordinate.

As the foremost representative of the Baroque style, Claudio Monteverdi led a revolution against the classical *ars perfecta* of the Netherlanders. He abandoned completely the vertical and horizontal unity gained by Cipriano in favor of a new structure, based, as we have seen, upon the dramatic implications of the text. At the same time, he created a new contrapuntal technique which was the basis for three and a half centuries of musical development. The new Baroque amphonic [7] style so clearly enunciated in Monteverdi's later works did not spring like Athena fully grown from the mind of the composer. Rather this style was the result of an evolution, and its basic elements can be found in Monteverdi's earliest works.[8] The "new counterpoint" is strongly foreshadowed in *Si ch'io vorrei morire*, and can best be seen in the musical treatment of the words "A questo bianco seno / Deh stringetemi fin ch'io venga meno" (measures 63–73). Throughout this section the top two voices act as a duet which is balanced against a voice in the lower parts serving to delineate the harmony of the duet. In this section there are essentially only two contrasted elements, the upper part or vehicle for the melody and the lower part giving harmonic support. (Two years later in Book V this new "counterpoint" was clarified with the inclusion of an obligatory *basso continuo* for six madrigals.) The structure of the "new counterpoint" is far easier to grasp than the old, for the ear has only two basic parts to understand instead of five.

The dramatic sense of the text carefully reinforced by this

7. Amphonic structure: a structure of basically two parts, melody and figured bass.
8. Schrade, in *Monteverdi*, very skillfully shows the steps of this evolution. My analysis is entirely based upon his work.

34

new and clear musical structure unites the madrigal into an easily understood whole. The textural coherence of Cipriano is replaced by a dramatic coherence underlaid by a clearly enunciated structure. This structure is built around a series of climaxes. The section treating the words "Ahi, car'e dolce lingua," for example, creates tension through dissonance and the steady rise of pitch. The tension reaches a climax on "Datemi tant'humore" and is gradually released as the music subsides on the following phrase, "Che di dolcezz' in questo sen m'estingua." As Schrade points out, this style is successful because it unifies technical structure with expression.[9] The madrigal continues on with this same pattern of climaxes, and ends on a regular musical *da capo* with the repetition of the opening phrase.[10] This new structure or system, clearer and more accessible than the old Renaissance style, has replaced the old style as a means of unifying the work.

Gesualdo's music falls between the extremes of these clearly enunciated styles. More completely even than Monteverdi, he breaks the vertical and horizontal unity achieved by Cipriano.[11] The horizontal unity of texture is destroyed by the sectionalization we have already noted. These small sections are composed in different styles, some chromatic, some rapid, some slow, some rhythmically intricate, some rhythmically regular, some contrapuntal, some chordal. Thus, in place of Cipriano's unbroken flowing texture, Gesualdo composes a number of short sections in different styles, which are set off from each other not only by their opposing styles but also by frequent rests for all the voices. In the forty-five measures which make up *Io parto*, there are ten points at which no voice sounds. Cipriano's carefully preserved rhythmical steadiness of the individual lines is undermined also by Gesualdo. The slow rhythm of one section changes abruptly to a very rapid pattern, as in measure 29. Within one section, Gesualdo shows a marvelous skill in composing extremely intricate and asymmetrical patterns such as that in his treatment of "con interroti omèi."

9. Schrade, p. 190.
10. Schrade discusses this madrigal at some length, and my discussion is based on his. Ibid., p. 193–96.
11. This break was not a sudden step taken by Gesualdo, but was the product of the evolution of the madrigal form up to Gesualdo's time.

There are some imitative sections, but these are always short, and their unifying effect is very slight.

The genius of Gesualdo, however, is revealed in his ability to achieve his remarkable effects while avoiding difficult jumps in the vocal line. There are no jumps of the forbidden tritone, or of sevenths or diminished sixths. Examination of the vocal lines shows that Gesualdo's "vocabulary" of intervals differs from Cipriano's only by the addition of the half-step interval, and the very occasional use of an octave jump. Despite the extreme chromaticism and the juxtaposition of unrelated chords, he manages to limit the individual lines to jumps of the third, the fourth, and the fifth, and, infrequently, the downward leap of a sixth. The effect of this careful technique is lost to the ear, however, because other, stronger factors break up any melodic unity which an individual part might have, or textural unity that the whole piece might have. Gesualdo's technique is discernible only in the score, and has thus escaped the notice of many critics. Although he still clung to the Renaissance theory of part writing in respect to intervals, he failed to achieve the unity which was the whole object of Renaissance refinement of technique. Gesualdo, then, developed no new technique. He developed an anticlassical style, but his technique remained firmly rooted in Renaissance counterpoint.

Gesualdo did not, therefore, adopt Monteverdi's "new counterpoint," nor did he employ the dramatic force of the text as an important unifying factor. The structure of *Io parto* is not one of climaxes, of tension and release, but rather one of subtle, unresolved tension, built up in various ways, and never convincingly resolved. Like Pontormo and Rosso, then, Gesualdo broke the systems governing the art of his day. His musical treatment made more obscure whatever logic his epigrammatic and paradoxical text may have had. Although his voice leading was conservative (and very skillful), his music fails to achieve and indeed makes no effort to achieve the classical ideal of Netherlandish polyphony. His short, almost abrupt sections have neither dramatic force nor an obvious musical structure to unite them.

There is, therefore, as strong a centrifugal or acentric tendency in Gesualdo's *Io parto* as there was in the two *Depositions*.

36

But as in the two paintings, this tendency is balanced by a complex, purely formed pattern holding the separate parts in place. Gesualdo was carrying out this formal, one could almost say surface, pattern in his treatment of the phrase "che il dolore / Privò di vita il core" which we have already discussed. Although not immediately apparent, there is a careful balancing of sections, chordal against polyphonic and rapid against slow. Stylistically, there are fourteen sections, and these are divided equally between chordal and polyphonic sections, sections that are relatively rapid and slower sections. These sections do not correspond to the structure of the text, but they do impose a formal sense of balance of their own on the music. This balance is so delicate that one gets the feeling that any movement, however slight, would send the structure toppling. Like the figures in Pontormo's *Deposition,* the almost atomistic sections of *Io parto* are held in place by a fine brittle surface pattern, difficult at first to perceive.

For the modern ear, the system that Gesualdo broke most obviously was the harmonic system. The juxtaposition of unrelated chords obtained by the almost constant use of the chromatic gender is as striking to ears accustomed to tonality as it was to those familiar with modality. Modality, properly considered, was a purely melodic phenomenon, however, and before we can discover how Gesualdo's music affected his contemporaries, we must first try to sketch in the position of harmony in the sixteenth century.[12] As soon as two voices were combined, purely melodic modal considerations had to be supplemented by conventions governing the harmony produced. At the beginning of the century, composers still thought largely in polyphonic linear terms, but by the end of the century, the seeds of tonality and its inherent harmonic implications had already taken root. Even in the Renaissance polyphonic style there were conventions which affected the harmony of the music, conventions which contemporary listeners expected, and which gave them the satisfying feeling that a given piece was firmly placed in one mode. Both in Renaissance and in Baroque music,

12. This issue is both difficult and controversial. The following discussion is only a sketch, because only points necessary to my later arguments have been included.

37

there was a sense of harmonic order, and even in the Renaissance the importance of remaining within the limits of a diatonic scale was much emphasized by theorists.

Certain features were established by convention within modality which helped the listener to recognize the mode in which any piece was written. Melodically, there were three important notes in the mode, corresponding to the perfect intervals. These were the *finalis*, or first degree, the *diatessaron*, and the *diapente*, the fourth and fifth respectively. The repetition of these tones, especially at important points, gave the piece its modal character.[13] The cadence, however, became an increasingly important indication of the mode of a piece. Gioseffe Zarlino, perhaps the foremost theorist of the sixteenth century, tells us that in judging the form of the mode of a piece, we should have "an eye to the cadences, which throw a great light on this question." [14] The formation of cadences was governed by certain conventions, originally based upon melodic considerations. The so-called Phrygian cadence arose naturally out of the voices leading step-wise to a consonant chord based on the finalis. An equivalent to what is now called the authentic or V-I cadence was formed by a slightly different treatment of leading tones with an octave jump on the fifth degree of the scale by the bass. The plagal or IV-I cadence was also a well-established convention by the sixteenth century.[15] As the century progressed, the latter two types of cadences came to dominate as the feeling for the importance of the fourth and fifth degrees increased.

Intervals, simultaneous as well as successive, were also considered by sixteenth-century musicians. Zarlino, in the *Institutione Harmoniche* of 1588, describes the canons governing vertical harmony and even harmonic progressions in some cases. He

13. "Note that what I call the form of the mode is the octave divided into its fifth and fourth, and that these two parts, arising from harmonic or arithmetic division, are heard repeated many times in their proper modes. Thus when we compose, we may know what is to guide us in leading the parts of our composition, and in putting the cadences at places suitable for the distinction of the words; as has been said, it is the mode." Zarlino, in Strunk, *Source Readings in Music History*, p. 255.

14. Ibid., p. 254.

15. That these three types of cadences were firmly established by Gesualdo's time has been confirmed by Janet Knapp and Claude Palisca, both members of the music faculty at Yale at the time of this writing.

had a clear idea of triads, both major and minor, although he did not use that exact word. In his discussion of the triad, he conceives of a root (bass note) with a third and fifth above it and describes this chord as the most pleasing: "On this variety [i.e. the combination of a major with a minor third] depend the whole diversity and perfection of harmonies. For, (as I shall say elsewhere) in the perfect composition, the fifth and third, or their extensions, must always be actively present." [16] Moreover, Zarlino warns the composer against false relations. Certain intervals are equally unacceptable whether they occur as a jump in one part or as succeeding notes in two different parts. These intervals are the tritone, major seventh, and augmented octave (diminished ninth). Thus the progression in example A is forbidden because of the tritone between the first note of the upper part and the second note of the lower.[17]

Example A:

Zarlino admits that in writing for many voices it may sometimes be necessary to violate this rule, but warns the composer that "when necessity compels him to offend, he ought at least to take care that he does so between diatonic steps, and in steps that are natural and proper to the mode." [18]

We may conclude from Zarlino's discussion that by 1558, even in the conservative Netherlandish tradition, the mode was being increasingly considered as a diatonic scale, and that composers were beginning to think in harmonic as well as melodic terms. The importance Zarlino assigns to cadences and his treatment of false relations are both symptoms of this tendency. In the realm of secular music, especially instrumental music, Professor Edward Lowinsky has found even more explicit evidence of harmonic and even tonal thinking.[19] A diatonic

16. Strunk, p. 242.
17. Ibid., pp. 238–40.
18. Ibid., p. 240.
19. Edward A. Lowinsky, *Tonality and Atonality in the Sixteenth Century* (Berkeley, University of California Press, 1961).

scale, be it modal, major, or minor, created a feeling of stability within a piece by giving it an harmonic system of reference to which the ear could grow accustomed.

It is only against this background of emerging harmonic thinking that works of this period may be understood. In the following discussion we are inevitably faced with a problem of vocabulary, for the music must be described, although the terms for description were not evolved until much later. Instead of inventing a new vocabulary for these musical phenomena, it seems more sensible to use conventional Rameauian terms, although admittedly composers of this period did not think in these terms. As we have seen, the concept of the triad, with a root, third, and fifth, was established in the thought of Zarlino, yet he did not possess these terms and had to express himself awkwardly. Therefore in the ensuing discussion, "modern" harmonic terms will be used for descriptive, but not analytical, purposes. These terms must be taken only as convenient names, not as part of a system of harmonic analysis evolved much later.

In Cipriano's madrigal, *Quando lieta sperai,* the mode does serve just this function of a diatonic scale. There are very few accidentals, and all but one are a result of sharping the G leading to A. The cadences [20] definitely emphasize the tone of A with a secondary emphasis upon the central step, E. Moreover, the majority of cadences are perfect, either plagal or authentic. Several are what modern terminology would call IV-V-I cadences. The cadence on "L'anim'ingombra" (example B) is an example of one of Cipriano's most "advanced" cadences. The harmony progresses from D to E to A, emphasizing the most important tones of the scale on A. Moreover, dissonance is used to increase the pull toward the final resolution on A. On the first beat of measure 19, a tritone appears in the upper two voices which is resolved when the cantus moves down to the A. This A in the cantus is then held over as a suspension in the E major triad which itself leads to an A triad. The important tones in this cadence, the D, the E, and especially the A, are emphasized by harmonic doubling, and the harmonic progression is outlined by the bass part. This

20. Cf. Cadence Chart, Appendix C, p. 99.

emphasis at the cadences upon A and upon related tones provides a constant point of reference which draws the piece together. As each phrase comes to rest at the proper place, via an accepted route, a sense of harmonic stability is created.

Monteverdi's harmonic structure is equally clear. As the cadence chart shows, there is a greater cadential emphasis upon the tonic of the scale, A, although less emphasis is placed upon the fourth and fifth degrees. There are more accidentals than in Cipriano's madrigal, but these can almost all be explained as leading tones to the tonic, dominant, and subdominant. The effect of these accidentals, however, is compensated by the almost exclusive use of authentic cadences, which, because of

Example B:

their uniformity, take on an even greater power as architectonic devices.

Although Monteverdi makes greater use of dissonance than did Cipriano, he always uses dissonance with a direction or purpose in mind. In cadences, the dissonances are directional, because they lead to a final resolution by creating a kind of tension which is resolved when the resolution is made. The long section treating the words "Ahi car'e dolce lingua / Datemi tant'humore / Che in dolcezz'in questo sen m'estingua" is merely an extension of this dramatic principle of tension and release. The first part of this section builds up tension with an increasing series of dissonances of sevenths and seconds, but, beginning with measure 27, this tension is gradually released. The effect of even so prolonged a dissonance is not to impair but to emphasize the final consonance or resolution.

The opening measures of *Io parto* will serve as an introduction to Gesualdo's treatment of harmony (see example C). The

41

piece opens on a repeatedly stated E major chord, followed without any preparation other than a rest by a D minor triad, also repeated. Then, moving down the interval of a third in the bass, Gesualdo introduces a B major chord on which he ends the cadence in the next measure after going back to an E minor triad. In the opening two measures, Gesualdo chooses with evident pleasure to leave two unrelated chords confronting each other across a rest. There is no attempt to mitigate the disturbing effect of this unusual progression. The next measure does bring some kind of order, but the E triad has become minor, and the effect of the stabilizing authentic cadence is severely limited. There follows a slow, very chromatic section of three measures on "che il dolore," ending with a cadence on an F♯ major triad. By the end of these opening six measures, all twelve tones of the chromatic scale [21] have been introduced, and the ear has lost all contact with the opening chord of E. The unifying force of a diatonic scale, used by both Cipriano and Monteverdi, has been abandoned. The system is broken or at least severely strained, and unrelated chords are juxtaposed in the boldest fashion.

Example C:

Gesualdo shows a far greater variation in the final chords of his cadences than either Cipriano or Monteverdi. There is a large increase in the number of cadences on chords unrelated to what seems to be the tonal center of the piece, E. The madrigal begins and ends with chords whose root is E, but the complex network of cadences in between can hardly be said to

21. Gesualdo was preceded in his chromatic and enharmonic experiments by Vicentino, whose enharmonic archicembalo he would have seen at Ferrara, and by Luzzazco Luzzazchi, who was also at Ferrara with Gesualdo.

bring the ear comfortably back to this point of reference. Furthermore, Gesualdo did not modulate, or, if one can say that he did, he modulates so often and to such remote keys that the ear cannot follow. There is an almost constant shifting from chord to chord, and each small shift fails to establish a key of its own.[22] Gesualdo's rule, opposite to that of either Cipriano or Monteverdi, seems to be never to stay in one place too long. Only once do succeeding cadences resolve themselves on the same chord, and the rest of the time the tonal center moves incessantly, keeping the ear lost, refusing the resting points which both Monteverdi and Cipriano were careful to provide. The result, as Alfred Einstein points out,[23] is a kind of musical nausea similar to the visual seasickness produced by Pontormo's painting.

Despite this constant motion, however, there is, on paper at least, a distinct but complex harmonic pattern. Although only audible to the most refined ear, the music, both in the cadences and between them, is centered around the tone of E. Nine of the sixteen cadences considered resolve on E or related chords. But Gesualdo does everything in his power to obscure even this harmonic structure. Cadential formulae, as we have seen, were important in both Cipriano and Monteverdi to bring the listener back to the desired center by a familiar route. Gesualdo uses conventional cadences to lead to resolutions unrelated to E, while he approaches E or related tones by thoroughly unconventional cadences. Gesualdo's unusual cadential technique needs to be examined in detail in order to appreciate how carefully he prevents the cadence from performing its usual function of bringing the listener back to a stable tonal center. The treatment of the phrase "Dunque ai dolore / Io resto" (measures 20–23) will serve as an excellent example.

The first cadence occurs in measure 21. In the preceding measure is a cadence on a C♯ major triad, followed by a jump

22. My personal opinion is that it is historically incorrect to talk of Gesualdo in terms of tonality when tonal music was just beginning to be written. At a time when the device of modulation had just been invented, it seems to me unrealistic to refer to Gesualdo as modulating every bar or so.

23. Einstein, *The Italian Madrigal*, p. 715.

to a triad on the fourth, F♯ major. The cadence in measure 21
ends on an F♯ minor triad in the first inversion. One would
have expected Gesualdo to have arrived at this chord through
an authentic cadence, C♯ major to F♯ minor. The Prince, however, progresses through a brief series of dissonances to a D
minor chord first inversion, and thence to a C minor chord,
also first inversion. From the C chord, he drops by thirds to A
minor, and finally to F♯ minor. This is certainly a long way
around. The effect of this complex harmonic motion is that one

Example D:

does not realize the close relation which actually exists between
the first and last chords. The second cadence ends on a C♯
minor triad, but instead of approaching this chord through its
fourth, the F♯ chord just stated, Gesualdo again travels a
strange route, via dissonances, chords of the first inversion,
and progressions by thirds. Harmonically, the effect is the same
as going on a long trip so confusing in its direction that the
traveler does not realize that he ended up just where he began.
What comprehensible harmonic outline there is is almost completely obscured.

Other details add to this effect of acentric instability. Of
the sixteen chords in these measures, fourteen are in the first
inversion. This position, as we have seen, was avoided by

44

Monteverdi and Cipriano in favor of the more stable position with the root in the bass. Moreover, the third is most often doubled, instead of the root or the fifth. This treatment, not used elsewhere in the madrigal, furthers the unsteadiness of the cadences (an ironic touch, considering that the text at this point is "Io resto"). A further element of instability is added by the fact that both of the cadences are feminine, resolved only on an unaccented beat. In measure 23, for instance, on the fourth beat (if a half note is taken as a beat in this measure), Gesualdo has an A seventh chord, leading, one would expect, to a D chord at the beginning of the next measure. Instead, he places a rest after the bar line, and brings the cadence to an inconclusive close on the last half of the fourth beat by introducing an F♯ in the Quintus, which forms the root of an F♯ major triad. The resolution of the next cadence on "Io resto" is likewise on an unaccented beat, and is hardly given a chance to sound before the vigorous motif on "Ah non fia mai" sweeps it away. A further instability is introduced at this cadence by the false relation existing between the Bass and Quintus on the first two beats of measure 23 and on the last beat of the preceding measure. This violates Zarlino's rule and even his admonition about exceptions.[24]

We have seen that both Monteverdi and Cipriano used dissonance only in a directional way, that is, leading to final resolution. In bar 20, Gesualdo places two biting dissonances on the last beat, as a transition between an F♯ major chord and a D minor. The dissonances are justified by the text, but there is no release of tension in a satisfying resolution; instead, Gesualdo proceeds to an unexpected chord which, although not dissonant itself, does not resolve the preceding dissonances in a normal way. Similarly, suspensions on the first two beats of measure 23 create E seventh chords which one would expect to resolve into an A chord. Instead, the cadence seems to fall on the last half of the second beat, with a C♯ minor chord in first inversion. A harmonic resolution is only obtained after all voices but two have left the phrase "Io resto" to begin a new section. Considered without this next section, the cadence

24. See p. 38 above.

is left unfinished. Unlike previous dissonances we have seen based on diatonic scales, Gesualdo's chromatic dissonances do not pull toward another chord, as Monteverdi's dominant seventh does, for example. Instead, by their very nature, these chords seem incapable of a resolution that can release the tension they create.

Gesualdo's cadences, then, do little to clarify the already obscure harmonic structure of his madrigal. All the details of his composition seem aimed at keeping the listener harmonically lost, in spite of the fact that there is a tonal center to the madrigal as a whole. Both Monteverdi and Cipriano were careful to establish diatonic scales which served as harmonic frameworks for their madrigals, frames of reference which made each madrigal easier to understand. Gesualdo abandons this clear system of diatonic scales, and therefore makes his madrigal difficult to understand harmonically.

Why? In almost every case, Gesualdo's harmonic technique is used for expressive purposes. Whereas Cipriano and Monteverdi expressed themselves within given harmonic systems, however different, Gesualdo achieved expression by breaking the system. His violently juxtaposed chords, his indefinite cadences, his shifting harmonic pattern all help to express the almost demented grief which is characteristic of all his madrigals.

This principle can be extended to the other aspects of the madrigal. Just as Rosso destroyed the element of psychological coherence in his *Deposition*, Gesualdo chose a text characterized by illogical paradoxes, and a total lack of any sensuous imagery which might help the listener to understand by providing a common frame of reference in the senses, as the pastoral imagery did in Cipriano's text. Cipriano expressed himself within the framework of Netherlandish polyphony; Gesualdo found expression by breaking this framework, by including very frequent rests for all voices, and chordal sections of simultaneous declamation. Monteverdi expressed himself within the bounds of a dramatic logic; Gesualdo did everything he could to obscure what little dramatic potential his text had. Monteverdi expressed himself within and almost by means of a strong musical structure; Gesualdo breaks the form of the madrigal into small pieces too numerous for the ear to grasp or place in any order.

46

All that remains is a purely formal delicate balance between sections of opposing textures and tempi. The text serves as a basis for musical fragmentation rather than unity. As in painting, expression is thought of in terms outside the usual frames of reference of the Renaissance and the Baroque. And it is in breaking through these systems that Gesualdo achieves his expression.

Because it is a system-breaking art, the art of Gesualdo, like that of Rosso and Pontormo, seems peculiar; there are no systems to help us understand. All three artists work in an abstract world, separated from the here and now, and the only real link is that of subjective emotion on the one hand, and an ultrarefined sensitivity for surface patterns on the other. Any structure seems imposed upon the material, rather than growing out of it naturally, as happened in the Baroque and the Renaissance. The connoisseur who can perceive the intricate formal patterns is all the more conscious of the skill of the artist in having imposed a pattern upon elements that in themselves have little cohesive force, either logically or formally. But the balance is always precarious, rife with potential disturbance. Therefore—even if we appreciate the complex surface patterns—disturbance, uneasiness, and tension convey the emotion at an almost psychological level.

The reason that the Mannerist work of art is acentric or centrifugal is that the parts are given. Rather than altering the various parts of his composition so that they naturally fit together, Gesualdo, like Rosso and Pontormo, seems to be dealing with fixed, immutable quantities which refuse to give up their own identity, but jostle each other uneasily within the complex formal pattern. The sections of *Io parto* have too much independence, and it is only with the greatest ingenuity that Gesualdo brings them all together. The difference between Monteverdi and Gesualdo is that one remade the elements into a new, and in many ways a stronger, form, while the other moved the pieces around still unchanged, until they formed a precarious balance. Monteverdi's forward-looking solution lasted for centuries; Gesualdo's retrospective rearrangement died with the composer, only to be revived when a similar art had come into fashion.

47

3 JOHN DONNE: MANNERIST STYLE IN THE MEDITATIVE GENRE

I n 1611, the same year that *Io parto* was published for
the first time, John Donne wrote *The First Anniversary,*
lamenting the death of a fifteen-year-old girl. The subject
matter of this long poem is peculiarly appropriate to the
present study, for Donne describes a world where the old order has been destroyed, but has not been replaced by any
new synthesis. The Medieval-Renaissance view of the unity of
the universe, the essential oneness of man, the earth, and the
heavens, has been broken by disrupting factors of which the
New Science is the chief culprit. As Marjorie Nicolson has
effectively pointed out,[1] the circle which characterized the old
view has been broken, and chaos is the result. There is in the
poem no trace of the unity which the New Science was to
achieve for seventeenth-century thought, a new order already
clearly visible in the work of Donne's contemporary, Francis
Bacon. Donne presents his reader with a picture of an orderless universe, where man's knowledge and power are severely
limited.

Our task, however, is to analyze *The First Anniversary* not
in content but in style. The element of style is less obvious in
poetry than in music, for unlike a musical composition, a
poem is conceptual in that it is made up of words which stand
for things or concepts. It might be useful to begin our discussion with a simple but fundamental distinction. Style, as
we have already noted, is the total effect produced by the way
in which an artist uses the materials of his craft. Professor
Marie Borroff, in the introduction to her critical study of *Sir
Gawain and the Green Knight,* echoes this definition when she
distinguishes style in literature as the way in which language
is used, the "how" of expressing anything in words as opposed
to the "what." [2]

Many scholars have examined "what" John Donne says in
The First Anniversary, but few have written about "how"

1. Marjorie Hope Nicolson, *The Breaking of the Circle* (Evanston,
Ill., Northwestern University Press, 1950).
2. Marie Borroff, *Sir Gawain and the Green Knight* (New Haven, Yale
University Press, 1962), p. 3.

Donne expresses himself. Interesting as the subject matter of the poem may be, here we shall confine our discussion almost entirely to style.

The First Anniversary, like several other contemporary poems, describes the decay of the world. This poem differs from others on the same theme in that Donne ascribes this catastrophe to an insignificant cause, the death of a young girl whom Donne had never seen. This basic proposition, that the death of Elizabeth Drury caused the decay of the entire universe, is not merely hyperbole, it is nonsense. It is not surprising that Ben Jonson remarked that *The First Anniversary* was "profane and full of blasphemies," and that "if it had been written of the Virgine Marie it had been something." [3] To this Donne replied, however, that "he described the Idea of a Woman and not as she was." Donne's reply, although it reveals the same tendency toward abstraction we have observed in other Mannerist artists, is actually of little help. Whether one considers Elizabeth Drury as Ideal Woman, as the Virgin, as Queen Elizabeth, or even, as some modern critics have maintained, as Astraea [4] makes little difference. The poem is constructed on a basic proposition which only ingenuity can defend; Donne gives us little clue. The controversy which has lasted from his day to ours only serves to underline the obscurity of the meaning of the poem.

In pursuance of our aim to examine style, we shall follow our previous pattern of considering each work in its context by comparing *The First Anniversary* to one Renaissance and one Baroque poem. Fortunately, since both Renaissance and Baroque have become acceptable terms in English literary criticism, it is easy to find poems belonging to each of these styles. John Donne laments the death of Elizabeth Drury. Sixteen years before, Edmund Spenser published an elegy on the death of Sir Philip Sidney, Spenser's great "paragon." *Astrophel,* as the elegy is called, is written in the pastoral tradition typical of the English Renaissance. In 1652, Richard Crashaw published *In the Glorious Assumption of Our Blessed Lady, The*

---

3. See Nicholson, *The Breaking of the Circle,* p. 67.

4. Marjorie Nicolson proposes Astraea as a partial solution to the riddle. Ibid., pp. 74–79.

Hymn,[5] which, unlike Donne's poem, is clear in its reference to the departure of the Virgin from the world. Crashaw writes in a new style which Austin Warren has effectively defined as Baroque.[6]

Astrophel is about the death of a young shepherd who, by symbolic transference, is identified with Sir Philip Sidney. In the course of the poem, all the conventions of the pastoral are observed, and the wistful atmosphere of Arcadia is evoked. Spenser is here working in a long-established genre begun in antiquity by Bion, Moscus, and Theocritus, a genre attractive to Spenser and many of his contemporaries because of the "easy affinity" which they felt with classical antiquity. Arcadia is primarily a sensual world, a world of trees and flowers, like Renaissance painting based on an abstraction of the most beautiful elements of the real world. Although Arcadia is not a realistic world in any sense, almost everything there has a tangible counterpart in common experience. Crashaw's world is furnished with similar elements. Seasons, flowers, forests, and trees are all mentioned, and these elements play the same role as in Spenser: [7] they indicate the emotions of either the speaker or the world. The earth in all its parts weeps for the loss of the Virgin.

If Crashaw's world is afflicted in body, Donne's world is afflicted in mind. Donne remained unresponsive to the pastoral genre which dominated the elegy at the time, and his poem is noticeably bare of the common trees and flowers found in both Spenser and Crashaw. The warm and vaguely sensuous world of Arcadia has been replaced by the cold, airless world of the conceit, by complicated arguments devoid of sensuous references. This fact alone shows Donne as possessing a sensibility somewhat different from that of Spenser or Crashaw. The sadness of the earth is expressed by winter in Crashaw, by cold winds and weeping waters. Donne's earth reflects the loss of Elizabeth Drury by the imperfection of its spherical form:

5. Referred to henceforth as *Hymn*.
6. Austin Warren, *Richard Crashaw: A Study in Baroque Sensibility* (Baton Rouge, La., Louisiana State University Press, 1939).
7. The same is true of the text for Cipriano's madrigal, *Quando lieta sperai*.

But keepes the earth her round proportion still?
Doth not a Tenarif, or higher Hill
Rise so high like a Rocke, that one might thinke
The floating Moone would shipwracke there, and sinke?

Before talking in more general terms, we must closely examine the prosody of each poet to discover how he uses the materials of his art to express his ideas. Because all the poems under discussion, especially *The First Anniversary*, are long, we must of necessity confine ourselves to a few representative lines in each. The opening lines of each poem will satisfactorily serve our purpose:

Spenser

Shepheards that wont on pipes of oaten reed,   1

Oft times [8] to plaine your loves concealed smart: 2

And with your piteous layes have learnd to breed   3

Compassion in a countrey lasses hart.   4

Hearken ye gentle shepheards to my song,   5

And place my dolefull plaint your plaints emong.   6

Crashaw

Hark! she is call'd, the parting houre is come   1

Take thy Farewell, poore world! Heav'n must goe home.   2

A peece of Heav'nly Earth; purer and brighter   3

Then the chast stars, whose choice lamps come to light her   4

While through the Christall orbes, clearer than they   5

She climbs; and makes a farre more milky way.   6

Donne

When that rich soule which to her Heaven is gone   1

Whom all they celebrate, who know they have one,   2

8. I use this sign to indicate a hovering accent, equally divided between two syllables. I have tried to distinguish between hovering accents and spondees, but in no case does this distinction affect my argument.

(For who is sure he hath a soule, unlesse   3

It see, and Iudge, and follow worthinesse,   4

And by Deedes praise it? He who doth not this   5

May lodge an In-mate soule, but tis not his.)   6

When that Queene ended here her progresse time,   7

And, as t'her standing house to heaven did clymbe,   8

Where, loth to make the Saints attend her long,   9

Shee's now a part of both the Quire, and Song,   10

This world, in that great earth-quake languished;   11

These short passages help to put Donne's style in context.
Spenser's verse here is flowing and musical. The metrical pattern is regular; the voice encounters little difficulty in imposing
the rhythm of iambic pentameter upon the verse. There are
several slight irregularities, to be sure, but these in no way
interrupt the flow of the words. These irregularities are the
hovering accent on "Oft times" (l. 2) and the placement of a
metrical accent upon such normally unaccented words as "in"
(l. 4) and "to" (l. 5). The effect of these variations of the
regular metrical pattern is rather to break the monotony of
the verse than to interfere seriously with its movement. Although Crashaw's verse is metrically far less regular than that
of Spenser, its flow is greater. In abandoning the steady rhythms
of Spenser, Crashaw created a new system of verse music, both
freer and stronger than Spenser's. Every variation in Crashaw's
first six lines is calculated to underline the meaning of the
words and enhance their force as pure sound. In the last two
lines, for example, the sound is of vital importance. The fifth
line ends with an enjambment, following the inversion of the
next-to-last foot. This inversion, along with the alliteration of
"Christall" and "clearer," emphasizes the latter word, and underlines the relation between the two. The use of alliteration again
on the last two words of line five, "than they," further increases
the appeal of the sound. The phrase "She climbs" at the beginning of line six is emphasized by its location at the beginning
of the line, and by the heavy spondaic movement of the first

foot. These purely musical devices, especially the use of enjambment, are skillfully employed to give the effect of climbing
in the sound of the verse.[9]

The regularity of his verse would seem to link Donne more
closely with Spenser than with Crashaw, for he makes little
use of the virtuoso manipulation of rhythms which the latter
poet employs. The first, third, fourth, fifth, and sixth lines
are relatively regular. The second line, however, suddenly interrupts the rhythm set up by the first:

> When that rich soule which to her Heaven is gone
> Whom all they celebrate, who know they have one,

An extra syllable is tacked onto the end of the line in an unaccented position. The word "one" has no place within the
rhythmic structure of the line, but hangs awkwardly on the
end. This is especially strange because the unaccented word
"one" is rhymed with the word "gone" in line 2. Unlike Spenser's minor irregularities, this line represents not a variation
but a breakdown of the pattern, a deliberate cacophony introduced by the poet. There are here very few of the musical
devices Crashaw used. Instead, the cacophonous effect is increased because the regular iambic pentameter which dominates
seems to exist only to emphasize the periodic violations of the
pattern.[10]

Because Spenser's words are to a large extent ordered syn-
tactically by the verse forms, his syntax is not particularly complex. The subject of the sentence, "Shepheards," is modified by
two subordinate clauses, each two lines long. There are two
predicates in the sentence, each occupying one line (lines five
and six). This structure is apparent after the first reading.
The structure of the stanza underlies the syntax, and makes
the sentence easier to understand. Crashaw's syntax, more rhetorical, is even simpler than Spenser's. His sentences are short
and structurally extremely simple. The first two lines of the
Hymn, for example, contain four complete thoughts in addition

9. Crashaw's verse music is discussed in greater detail below, pp. 109–
10.

10. This analysis of Donne's prosody applies only to *The First Anniversary*, and perhaps to a few other poems written around 1610. Donne's
later style, especially that of the Holy Sonnets, has much more in common with Crashaw's style.

to the exclamation "Hark!" There are two subordinate clauses, but each of these is short, and the sentence structure remains obvious.

Donne's syntax is infinitely more complex. The first six lines are not even a complete sentence, but are merely one long elliptical [11] subordinate clause beginning with "When." The sentence does not end until line eleven, and even there one finds only a semicolon. The syntactical structure inside the opening six lines resembles a nest of Chinese boxes in its intricacy. The second half of the first line contains a subordinate clause modifying "soule," and lines two through six are another subordinate clause modifying "soule." Within this clause, in the second part of line two, is yet another subordinate clause, this time modifying "all" (line two). The parenthetical expression (lines three through six) explains the clause beginning "Whom all they celebrate," but this section itself contains a complete question and answer, each of which in turn contains one or more subordinate clauses. If an unfortunate eighth-grade student were told to analyze Donne's first sentence by circling all subordinate clauses and connecting each with the word it modifies, the clause "who doth not this" (line five) would have four circles around it. This extreme complexity makes the sentence excessively hard to follow, and one must re-read the lines several times to see how they fit together.

This increased syntactical complexity reflects a meaning which is far more concentrated than that of either Crashaw or Spenser. In his first stanza, Spenser is content simply to evoke the pastoral atmosphere, to begin a formal type of introduction, identifying his poem with the laments of the Arcadian shepherds. His meaning may be easily paraphrased. Because of his numerous repeats, Crashaw's meaning is equally plain. Crashaw constantly repeats and elaborates on the same thought. In lines one and two, for example, the four separate clauses express the same theme in a different way: The Virgin has been called to Heaven.

No sooner does Donne begin, however, than he becomes immediately entangled in a complex "metaphysical" debate which occupies his attention to the end of line six. Lines three to six

11. There is no verb in this clause.

contain an extremely condensed statement of a complex theory, which Donne's intricate syntax manages to squeeze into a remarkably short space. A paraphrase of the first six lines would be considerably longer than the original statement, for no details can be omitted without ruining the argument. We shall borrow the verb from line 11: "The world languished as an earthquake when that rich soul (Elizabeth Drury) went to Heaven. All men who have a soul themselves revere her soul. How can we be sure that we have a soul, unless it responds to the beauty in other souls by seeing, judging, and finally praising this worthiness by deeds? If we do not experience this response, our body may house a soul, but it is not ours." In contrast to Spenser, Donne presents his reader immediately with an intricate argument. Moreover, as in all his poetry, Donne takes pleasure in expressing this complicated idea in a very condensed epigrammatic style, squeezed into four lines. The parts of the argument are gathered and put together in the most intricate and compressed way imaginable.

Two distinct tendencies emerge, then. We have seen that both Crashaw and Spenser were more interested in their prosody than was Donne. Although Spenser was inclined to ordered regularity, and Crashaw to dramatic irregularity, both were striving for certain effects in verse. Donne, on the other hand, seemed to ignore the possibilities of the verse, and the iambic pentameter he employs is more a formality for him than an organically important part of the poem. Conversely, Spenser and Crashaw both employ rather simple syntax, and their meaning is therefore relatively clear. Donne's syntax is much more complex, and his economical verse contains an intensity and complexity of meaning which are absent in the other two poets.

We should note in passing yet another difference between the three poets. The first lines of a poem are important because they set the tone for the rest of the poem; they introduce the reader to the subject. Spenser employs a formal introduction which is not an integral part of the rest of the poem. He uses words which would have evoked in the mind of the Renaissance reader the whole atmosphere of the pastoral. Crashaw and

Donne both go directly to the point. Crashaw in fact states the theme of the poem over and over, elaborating on it each time in a kind of virtuoso display. The poem thus has a focus all the way through. Donne characteristically gets sidetracked into a subsidiary argument before he can finish the first statement of his theme. Crashaw's repetitions make his opening statement abundantly clear; Donne's involved parenthetical argument takes the force and focus out of the entire opening of his poem. The reader is not sure where Donne is going, for this complex argument interrupts the flow of the thought just as surely as the metrical irregularities interrupted the flow of the sound.

The opening passage of *The First Anniversary* gives us a good indication of Donne's style. We have seen how he turned away from the pastoral tradition in the elegy, and in so doing turned away also from the Renaissance style of poetry as exemplified by Spenser. For relative simplicity, clarity, and order, he has everywhere substituted intricacy, complexity, and tension. The more closely one examines the poem, the more these factors reveal themselves. In breaking the metrical regularity, Donne does not mold his verse into new, more sonorous musical patterns as Crashaw did, but moves instead toward cacophony. An extraordinarily complex meaning is expressed by an intricate syntax and in verse characterized by uneasy tension.

I have already suggested that Crashaw, while breaking from the regular metrical system of Spenser, did so only to establish his own system based upon verse music. Austin Warren, in his study of Crashaw, defines music in verse thus:

> Commonly poetry is said to be "musical" when it avoids hiatus, harsh combinations of consonants, and explosive "stops," and eschews abrupt shifts of rhythm; when it makes large use of "liquids" and sonorous vowels and feminine rhyme; when by the employment of consonantal and vowel sequences, word glides into word as though, independent of the sense, sounds had a magnetism of their own.[12]

12. Warren, *Richard Crashaw*, p. 108.

Spenser uses these devices often. His regular meter contributes to the musical effect, as do such devices as alliteration and consonance:

> With dolours dart for death of Astrophel.
> Out of his lips like lillies pale and soft.

The first lines illustrate Spenser's technique of controlling the stops in a line, for by bringing the hard consonant d into a pattern by its repetition, Spenser limits its power to interrupt the flow of the verse. The second example is a concert of sibilants and soft vowels, the sounds of which do have "a magnetism of their own." Spenser also repeats whole words to increase the music of his verse:

> *Stella* the faire, the fairest star in skie,
> As faire as Venus or the fairest faire:

As Austin Warren has pointed out, Crashaw makes far greater use of these musical devices than does Spenser. He breaks the regular meter only to establish new sound patterns more compelling than the old. In the *Hymn*, the variations in rhythm are carefully controlled to produce the desired effect, as we have already seen. Throughout the poem, Crashaw makes constant use of consonance and assonance, and repeats whole phrases frequently. The use of a refrain is itself an indication of an interest in sound. Moreover, the refrain of the *Hymn* well illustrates Crashaw's technique:

> Come away my love,
> Come away my dove, Cast off delay:
> The Court of Heav'n is come
> To waite upon thee home; Come, come away.

This passage derives its effect from the use of repetition, the frequent alliteration, and the rich rhyming scheme.

In comparision to the verse music of Crashaw or even of Spenser, Donne's poetry sounds thin. The very first line contains a difficult consonant combination—"rich soule"—which, according to Warren, musical verse should avoid. Donne makes very sparing use of such devices as consonance and assonance.

60

His rhymes are not as perfect as Crashaw's nor does he often repeat rhyming pairs, as does Crashaw. (Much of the rhyming scheme in the *Hymn* is built upon the words "they," "way," "stay," and "delay.") In breaking Spenser's regular metrical pattern, Donne neglected the potential for rich and sonorous verse music which freedom from this pattern offered to Crashaw.

This lack of sensuous appreciation for the sound of words is the reflection of an entire sensibility. We have seen that Donne remained unaffected by the whole pastoral tradition whereas Spenser used the pastoral mode in four of his six poems on the death of Sir Philip Sidney. What made Donne reject and Spenser adopt the pastoral was a difference in sensibility between the two. The characteristics of the Arcadian atmosphere appealed to Spenser; he mentions such details as oaten reeds, country lasses, grassy banks, and nymphs. The evocation of this atmosphere was obviously pleasing to the poet, and he assumed that it would likewise be pleasing to his audience; Arcadia is a pleasant, classically inspired land where justice and order reigned, where the most handsome and valorous shepherd always makes love to the most beautiful shepherdess. This world would naturally appeal to the Renaissance mind as exemplifying a satisfying order. It did not, however, appeal to Donne. There is no mention of this Arcadian world; indeed any of the elements which make up Arcadia would be completely out of place in *The First Anniversary*.

Two selected passages may give us an example of the sensibilities of each poet. Each passage contains a description of heaven which indicates the characteristics of each poet's imagination.

Spenser: Ah no: it is not dead, ne can it die,
   But lives for aie, in blisfull Paradise:
   Where like a new-borne babe it soft doth lie,
   In bed of lillies wrapt in tender wise,
    And compast all about with roses sweet,
    And daintie violets from head to feet.

   There thousand birds all of celestiall brood
   To him do sweetly caroll day and night:

61

Donne: When that Queene ended here her progresse time,
         And, as t'her standing house, to heaven did clymbe,
         Where, loth to make the Saints attend her long,
         Shee's now a part of both the Quire, and Song,
         This world, in that great earth-quake languished;

The language used by these two poets is significant. Both Spenser and Donne see Heaven as blissful paradise, but beyond that their visions differ. Spenser thinks of a "new-borne babe" lying "soft" in Paradise, tenderly wrapt in a bed of lilies, surrounded by roses and violets, and sweetly caroled by birds. All the senses save taste are satisfied by this vision of Heaven— the eye, the ear, the nose, the touch. The vision is concrete, and, in many ways, worldly; the delights imagined are drawn from earthly sensual delights. Donne does not describe Heaven in detail, but tries instead to fix in the reader's mind the relation between heaven, earth, and Elizabeth Drury. This he accomplishes by means of two metaphors. In the first, Elizabeth Drury is compared to a queen whose home and governing seat is Heaven, but who is temporarily on a "progresse" on earth. It is important to note that this metaphor calls up an idea which is purely cerebral; one cannot smell, or see, or hear Heaven, as one could the flowers and the birds. The second metaphor would seem at first more sensuous, for it at least involves music. The "Quire, and Song," however, have little to do with audible sounds. The "Quire" is the Choir of Saints or the Church Triumphant which praises God in Heaven, and the "Song" refers to the perfect harmony of God in which all heavenly creatures participate. Donne is here expressing a mystical doctrine which would hold that Elizabeth Drury, although absorbed in the heavenly "music" or perfection, could still retain her identity and contemplate this perfection as a spectator.[13] The "Quire, and Song," then, are very different from Spenser's choir of birds, and reveal a very different sensibility.

Although Crashaw is usually considered one of the Metaphysical poets, in sensibility as in verse music, he lies far

13. Clay Hunt, *Donne's Poetry* (New Haven, Yale University Press, 1956), pp. 97–100.

closer to Spenser than he does to Donne. That these two elements should be closely linked is not surprising, for it is just
the poet who appreciates sensuous images who also appreciates
the melodic sounds of which verse is capable. The sensuousness
of Crashaw's imagery is obvious. Even a glance through the
Hymn shows us that Crashaw's sensibility is extremely sensuous; he uses material objects to praise the divine goodness:
"sweetest showers," "fairest flow'rs." Both Crashaw and Donne
mention the stars. Donne considers them in an astronomical or
astrological sense; he draws upon such characteristics as their
motion, and their influence upon the earth. Crashaw centers
his attention elsewhere. He mentions that the stars are pure
and chaste, but links this moral quality with a physical one.
"Purer and brighter" are the stars, they are "choice lamps,"
"Christall orbes"; they are "clear" and they "light her."
Whereas Crashaw emphasizes their impression on the senses,
Donne concentrates on their attributes as perceived by the mind.
In comparison to either Crashaw or Spenser, Donne avoids
calling on the senses of the reader. His world is an abstract one,
divorced from the everyday world of the senses. The world
of *The First Anniversary* is deliberately hard to penetrate, so
that only the most clever may divine its meaning. There is no
easy frame of reference set up to draw the reader into the world
of the poem.

We might note in passing that this clearly indicates a pre-
supposition about the nature of poetry. Art which is hidden,
involved, in which the meaning is difficult to penetrate, is by
some men and by some ages held to be better, higher, and
nobler than that which is immediately comprehensible. In the
Middle Ages or the Renaissance the meaning was often hidden
under allegories or "dark conceits," but for Donne, and for
those like him, there is no allegory, only a baffling density of
ingenious and intellectual comparisons.

No discussion of John Donne would therefore be complete
without some consideration of the metaphysical conceit. Both
Crashaw and Donne abandoned the conventional Renaissance
imagery, which they felt was outworn. The metaphors of both
are startling. However, as our discussion of sensibility would
suggest, Crashaw retained the senses as the basis for his im-

agery, which was consequently easily accessible; Donne based his imagery on abstract, purely intellectual relationships, and his poetry is therefore far less accessible.

Spenser makes a good starting point for this investigation, for it is against the Renaissance that the Metaphysicals reacted. Spenser's *Astrophel* is not rich in imagery, but what imagery there is is conventional, and depends for the most part upon similarities discernible by the senses:

> Her yellow locks that shone so bright and long,
> As Sunny beames in fairest somers day:
>
> And with sweet kisses suckt the wasting breath,
> Out of his lips like lillies pale and soft.

These figures are not functional, but decorative. The sunny beams and pale lilies relate to the rest of the poem insofar as they are part of the natural world of Arcadia. There is no more than a surface resemblance between sun and hair, lips and lilies. The elements compared either look alike or feel alike; there is no similarity of basic nature or function. Other metaphors in the poem are similarly based on the senses:

> His sports were faire, his ioyance innocent,
> Sweet without sowre, and honny without gall:

Astrophel's music is compared with that of the summer lark (l. 33), and Astrophel's love, Stella, with the stars. (Here again Spenser, like Crashaw, selects the visual qualities of the star, as opposed to Donne's use of abstractions.) Spenser's images, then, are both highly visualized and decorative.

In Crashaw, we note several images very similar to those we found in Spenser. For example, the Virgin, like Stella, is compared to a star. The *Hymn* has few "conceits," however, and in this sparsity it is unlike the majority of Crashaw's poems. Perhaps his most famous poem is *The Weepers*. The subject of this thirty-one-stanza poem is the weeping Magdalen, but Crashaw restricts his discussion to only her eyes, her cheeks, her tears, and so on. His first verse is indicative of the rest.

> Hail, Sister Springs,
> Parents of Silver-forded rills!
> Ever bubling things!
> Thawing Chrystall! Snowy hills,
> Still spending, never spent; I meane
> Thy faire eyes, sweet *Magdalen.*

Here and throughout the poem, Crashaw concentrates on the sensual qualities of the eyes themselves, and their tears. The entire poem is in one sense merely decorative, for such metaphors as the "silver springs" are totally irrelevant to the context of the Magdalen. Mary Magdalen herself has disappeared by the end of the poem; only her tears and eyes remain. The profuse shower of imagery so overdecorates the poem that the sense is lost. Admittedly, this is an extreme example, but it is an extreme example of Crashaw's usual style. As we look back from the vantage point of *The Weepers* on Spenser's *Astrophel,* we see that Crashaw has adopted and exaggerated Spenser's imagistic technique. *The Weepers* represents a fantastic series of images that are Spenser's sensuous and decorative images pushed to their utmost limit; they are a virtuoso display in sensuous decoration.

While Donne rejected the conventionality of Spenser's metaphors, he did so in a way very different from Crashaw. Just after the famous and oft-quoted section on the "New Philosophy," Donne compares Elizabeth Drury to magnetism. This comparison is every bit as startling as any of Crashaw's conceits.

> This is the worlds condition now, and now
> She that should all parts to reunion bow,
> She that had all Magnetique force alone,
> To draw, and fasten sundred parts in one;
> She whom wise nature had invented then
> When she observ'd that every sort of men
> Did in their voyage in this worlds Sea stray,
> And needed a new compasse for their way;

The comparison here goes from the palpable (Elizabeth Drury) to the impalpable (magnetism). Donne's image is more abstract than its subject, for magnetism is a purely mental construct which cannot be seen, heard, touched, smelled, or tasted. The

65

similarity is one of function. In the world of men, Elizabeth Drury brought order, which subordinated "Prince, Subiect, Father, and Son" into a hierarchy. Indeed, Donne has just finished lamenting the breakdown of this hierarchical society (ll. 215–18). Just as Elizabeth Drury united men, so a magnet draws and fastens pieces of metal to it. Donne, however, immediately extends this metaphor into the moral sphere. Just as men receive direction from the world's magnetic force acting on their compass needles as they stray "in this worlds Sea," so Elizabeth Drury gave moral direction to men before she died. What forms the basis for the comparison is not a sensuous or palpable relation, but the similarity of *function* between Elizabeth Drury and magnetic force. Donne in no way visualizes this, for he does not refer to a lodestone, which one could picture, but instead talks of magnetism in general. The single most striking fact about all the imagery of *The First Anniversary* is that none of it is based on a relationship perceivable only by the senses.

Another difference may be seen between this metaphor of the magnet and the several metaphors we have just examined. Neither Spenser's lily lips nor Crashaw's "Portable and compendious Oceans" had any real relevance to the structure of the poem as a whole. They fit in their respective poems only through the things they are compared with, and not on their own account. It is a different matter with Donne's metaphor. In the first place, the entire poem is built up around the analogy between the three worlds, the little world of man, the earth, and the heavens. Moreover, he speaks elsewhere of these worlds in both physical and moral terms, and shifts abruptly from one sense to the other.[14] Lines 53 and 54 draw the analogy that Elizabeth Drury is to the world as the soul is to man. This metaphor stuck in the poet's mind, for at the beginning of *The Second Anniversary*, he expands upon it. William Harvey, moreover, considers magnetism the soul of the earth, and this figure had become a convention.[15] Thus all the elements for Donne's

14. After describing the imperfection of the earth's physical features (ll. 285–301), Donne abruptly shifts to the moral sphere:

> Are these but warts, and pock-holes in the face
> Of th'earth? Thinke so: but yet confesse, in this
> The worlds proportion disfigured is,
> That these two legges whereon it doth relie,
> Reward and punishment are bent awrie.

metaphor were before him. The metaphor itself is as tightly bound up in the general structure of the poem as one could possibly imagine. It echoes a previous metaphor, it fits in perfectly with the three-circle pattern of the poem, and it operates on both a moral and a physical level.

Although it carries a moral implication, the metaphor is not philosophically consistent with the rest of the poem, for it depends upon the very analogies which it is the purpose of the poem to destroy. *The First Anniversary* describes the collapse of the old unity which had previously embraced man, earth, and Heaven, but Donne bases much of his imagery upon the correspondences of these three "worlds." In this light, the very intricate and tightly woven metaphoric structure can be seen as a kind of formal pattern, not organically but mechanically linked to the subject matter of the poem.

This intricate and formal pattern is characteristic of the structure of the poem as a whole. As we have seen in our examination of music and art, one of the most important elements of style is structure. All artists are faced with the problem of uniting the various parts of their work into a unified whole. The problem of unity is of particular interest to the Mannerist artist, because, as we have seen, the parts of a Mannerist work of art seem to resist any structure imposed upon them.

For Spenser, the main unit of organization is the stanza. The six-line stanza of *Astrophel* is carefully ordered. Take, for example, the second stanza:

> To you alone I sing this mournfull verse,
> The mournfulst verse that ever man heard tell:
> To you whose softened hearts it may empierse,
> With dolours dart for death of *Astrophel*.
> To you I sing and to none other wight
> For well I wot my rymes bene rudely dight.

The rhyme scheme, ABABCC, reflects the structure of the verse, for there are two units, the first of four and the other of two lines. The four-line group may be divided into two sections of

15. Nicolson, *The Breaking of the Circle*, pp. 122–26. Louis Martz further points out that Southwell and others had established the convention of referring to the Virgin Mary as the magnetic force in the world: *The Poetry of Meditation* (New Haven, Yale University Press, 1954), p. 232 n.

two lines each, and each of these two-line sentences has the same thought structure, the first line announcing the singing of the song, and the second expanding on the sadness of the song. The last couplet sums up the first four lines, and gives a general comment. It, too, reflects the structure of the two-line unit, for the first line of the last couplet talks of the singing of the song and the last of the song itself. This structure is emphasized by the repetition of the phrase "To you" at the beginning of each two-line sentence. Within the unit of the stanza, the thought is carefully organized and structured so that it seems to fall naturally into symmetrical and readily discernible patterns.

The organization of the poem as a whole is held together by the thread of the narrative. At the end of *Astrophel*, however, the narrative is replaced by the lament of Astrophel's sister, Clorinda. If we except the two stanzas at the end, which form a transition to the next poem, the lament is sixteen stanzas long. The first eight stanzas are a lament over the sadness of the speaker (four stanzas) and the unhappy state of the earth (four stanzas). Within the first four stanzas, the first asks a question, and the other three all offer answers, only the last of which is accepted. We find at least a tendency toward the same symmetrical, hierarchical order which we found in the stanza.

Crashaw's structure is plainly not the symmetrical, carefully constructed order of Spenser; it is rather a far freer structure making itself felt, as one would expect, through the sound of the verse. The structure is centered around climaxes which are audible when the verse is read aloud, climaxes in the sound of the poem whch reflect focal points in the thought. The major climax of the poem occurs on line 37. Before this point, Crashaw has set up a kind of tension between the desire of Heaven for the Virgin to leave the world and the reluctance of earth to have her go. The intensity of the verse is increased as the plea of Heaven is repeated in the refrain. Starting in line 33, the rhythm gets more agitated, as the answer to the question, "Will she goe?" is given three times. Finally, the spondaic line 37 releases both the tension in the thought, and that in the sound.

> Come away my love,
> Come away my dove, Cast off delay:

> The Court of Heav'n is come
> To waite upon thee home; Come, come away.
> She's call'd again. And will she goe?
> When Heav'n bidds come, who can say No?
> Heav'n calls her, and she must away,
> Heav'n will not, and she cannot stay.
> Goe then; goe (*glorious*) on the golden wings

The rest of the hymn is an ecstatic paean to the Virgin which itself reaches a lesser climax in lines 58 and 59. The structure in the *Hymn* is centered around climaxes of thought and sound. The poem is short enough that the effect of these climaxes can be felt throughout the work. This structure, although freer and more flowing than that of Spenser, is nevertheless effective in unifying the poem.

Donne uses no stanza form. In contrast to Spenser, he pays little attention to the verse form, for his thought moves on independently of the structure of the line. He seldom makes an effort to confine one thought to a line. His sentences and clauses spill from one line to the next, and the rhyming iambic couplets remain an essentially artificial form imposed upon the subject matter. This characteristic contrasts strongly with the poems of Crashaw and Spenser in which the structure seems to grow naturally out of the material.

If we are to find a significant structure, then, we must turn to the poem as a whole. Louis Martz has carefully and capably analyzed the organization of *The First Anniversary* in relation to a well-developed tradition of meditation in European literature.[16] According to Martz, the poem can be broken down into a number of divisions and subdivisions. His analysis will give us an overall summary of the meaning of the poem, as well as a clear outline of its structure:

Introduction, 1–90. The world is sick, "yea, dead, yea putrified," since she, its "intrinsique Balme" and "preservative," its prime example of Virtue, is dead.

Section I, 91–190: "how poore a trifling thing man is."

16. *The Poetry of Meditation*, pp. 221–28.

1. Meditation, 91–170. Because of Orignial Sin man has decayed in length of life, in physical size, in mental capacity.
2. Eulogy, 171–82. The girl was perfect virtue; she purified herself and had a purifying power over all.
3. Refrain and Moral, 183–90. Our only hope is in religion.

Section II, 191–246: "how lame a cripple this world is."

1. Meditation, 191–218. The "universall frame" has received injury from the sin of the Angels, and now in universe, in state, in family, " 'Tis all in pieces, all cohaerence gone."
2. Eulogy, 219–36. Only this girl possessed the power which might have unified the world.
3. Refrain and moral, 237–46. Contemn and avoid this sick world.

Section III, 247–338: "how ugly a monster this world is."

1. Meditation, 247–304. Proportion, the prime ingredient of beauty, no longer exists in the universe.
2. Eulogy, 305–24. The girl was the "measure of all Symmetree" and harmony.
3. Refrain and Moral, 325–38. Human acts must be "done fitly'nd in proportion."

Section IV, 339–76: "how wan a Ghost this our world is."

1. Meditation, 339–58. "Beauties other second Element, / Colour, and lustre now, is as neere spent."
2. Eulogy, 359–68. The girl had the perfection of color and gave color to the world.
3. Refrain and Moral, 369–76. There is no pleasure in an ugly world; it is wicked to use false colors.

Section V, 377–434; "how drie a Cinder this world is."

1. Meditation, 377–98. Physical "influence" of the heavens upon the earth has been weakened.
2. Eulogy, 399–426. The girl's virtue has little effect on us now because of this weakened "correspondence" between heavens and earth; in fact the world's corruption weakened her effect while she lived.
3. Refrain and Moral, 427–34. Nothing "Is worth our

travaile, grief, or perishing," except the joys of religious virtue.

Conclusion, 435–74.[17]

Several structural characteristics emerge from this analysis. The first is that *The First Anniversary*, in spite of its first impression as a long, rambling poem, is based on a very intricate pattern. It consists of five sections and an introduction and conclusion. Each of these sections is separated from the others by a kind of refrain, and each section in turn breaks itself down into three subsections, a meditation, a eulogy, and a moral. This structure, based on traditional forms in religious meditation, is far more complex than that in Spenser or Crashaw. Indeed it is so complex that it is not effective inside the poem; the refrains are too far apart to really make themselves felt as a binding organizational force. The pattern is a cerebral order, opposite in nature to Crashaw's free and organic pattern based on climaxes. Moreover, unlike Spenser's order, this structure is not symmetrical or hierarchical. The sections are not of equal length, and there are too many of them of equal importance. The mind cannot "read" [18] these seven parts, irregularly spaced. The order is not apparent; it is discernible. Donne here seems to be pursuing form as an end in itself, clinging to a traditional scheme of which he does not make full use. His intricate pattern does not bear fruit.[19]

Formally, then, this structure does not succeed in unifying the poem because it is so complex. This failure might have been overcome if Donne had bound the poem into a tight unit logically, but such is not the case, and the problem lies where we began our investigation of Donne. The basic proposition, upon which the entire poem is based, does not succeed, for Elizabeth Drury cannot be the cause of the ills which Donne enumerates. This cause-and-effect relationship should be the binding element in the poem, uniting each meditation with its eulogy and moral. Within these smaller units, Donne is ex-

17. Ibid., pp. 222–23.
18. In the same way the eye cannot "read" the intricate surface patterns in the *Depositions* of Pontormo and Il Rosso.
19. Clay Hunt finds the same tendency in Donne's *Hymne to God, My God, in My Sickness*. See *Donne's Poetry*, pp. 191–93.

quisitely logical, and yet the poem as a whole is illogical. For example, in attributing the decay of man since the age of giants to the recent death of a small girl, Donne is simply not making sense. Because the basic proposition is illogical, there is no "cyment" to bind together these parts, and the transitions between them are awkward:

> This man, so great, that all that is, is his
> Oh what a trifle, and poore thing he is!
> If man were any thing, he's nothing now:

As the poem progresses, the hyperbole becomes more and more strained. A logical tension is naturally set up between the great effect, cited in the meditations, and the trifling cause on which Donne tries to expand in the eulogies. It is this tension, this illogicality, that Martz criticizes.[20] At the very center of the poem, its basic proposition, is a manifest absurdity.

It is easy to argue that this is simply bad poetry because it does not fit together. The same type of criticism was the standard one aimed at Mannerist painting. One question, however, remains unsolved by this argument. Why did Donne write the poem and publish it? Surely another type of elegy less absurd would have pleased Robert Drury, his patron, and would have provided him with "rent" enough. Donne remains today one of the most capable, complicated, and subtle thinkers ever to write English poetry. His intricate and ingenious arguments are unparalleled. That he did not see the absurdity of the argument that underlies his poem is inconceivable.

One must conclude that Donne purposely based his poem on an enigma so difficult that it has not been satisfactorily solved in the three and a half centuries since the poem was written. He leaves the reader with a long and disjointed threnody, the complex formal structure of which seems artificially imposed upon the subject matter. The sections of this long poem do not fit naturally together, but are held in a kind of uneasy balance by the formal structure.

20. *The Poetry of Meditation*, pp. 228–33.

4 SOME CONCLUSIONS

H aving thus surveyed four works of art in three art forms, we are now in a position to return to some of the questions posed at the outset of our study. In practical terms, the justification for introducing the concept of Mannerism into literary and musical criticism depends upon whether or not there are works in these fields, the style of which cannot adequately be described by the already established terms of Renaissance and Baroque or, in the special case of English literature, by the term Metaphysical.[1]

Part of our task has been to establish that the four works, while sharing common stylistic features, differ substantially in style from works accepted as Renaissance or Baroque. In summing up our evidence for this point, however, we must attempt to go beyond the language of style, to divine the deeper meaning, to reconstruct the basic elements of the mood common to Pontormo, Rosso, Gesualdo, and Donne.

In comparison to the artists of the surrounding periods, the work of Rosso and Pontormo, of Gesualdo and Donne, seems rough or crude. In all of them the technique is usually designed to call attention to itself. In painting this crudeness is shown in the modeling of figures, the treatment of colors, the handling of space, and the apparent lack of proportion. In his jagged and unprepared harmonic changes and numerous abrupt stops, Gesualdo's technique appears equally harsh. Donne's style, too, is deliberately rough in comparison with Spenser's or Crashaw's. As Ben Jonson remarked, "Jack Donne, for not keeping meter, deserves hanging." The flow of his verse is interrupted by occasional irregular lines or harsh sounds which give a jerky, uneven effect. In all three art forms any sense of smoothness or flow is purposely destroyed.

1. One of the ablest treatments of the term *Metaphysical* is by Frank J. Warnke. Mr. Warnke distinguishes the Metaphysical from the "High Baroque" by observing that the latter style "is more a hyperextension of Renaissance techniques than a revolt against these techniques." *European Metaphysical Poetry* (New Haven, Yale University Press, 1961), p. 3. As John Donne represents a revolt against Renaissance techniques, his style seems to me fundamentally different from any Baroque style.

These four artists also shared a similar tendency to divorce their art from the common-sense world. References to the senses were especially avoided, and the result is the impression in each case of a world more abstract than the worlds of either the Renaissance or the Baroque. One of the most noticeable qualities in each of the Baroque works we have looked at is a new sense of declamation and of drama. By these devices, along with the unification of this new expressive quality with the technical structure, the Baroque artist brought even the most supernatural event into the realm of human experience. Everything is expressed by ordinary people, in the tones of natural speech, and with imagery taken from the common experience of the senses. The only change is the nonessential one of exaggeration. Drama was for the first time psychologically understandable because it represented the interplay of emotions of normal people. The Mannerist artist did the opposite, treating the natural in terms of the supernatural. The logic is never clear, and few figures or images are taken from the realm of common sense. Instead, the relations between the elements of the work seem to be governed by a supernatural order, an order both complex and delicate, and never fully comprehensible. Speech is artificial or researched, and convincing movement or drama is impossible because there are no apparent rules to govern either motion or emotion.[2]

The effects upon which part of the impact of Mannerist art depends are the result of the violent yoking together of apparently unrelated elements. The color and space of Pontormo and Rosso, the harmony of Gesualdo, and the imagery of Donne are all examples of the pleasure these artists take in startling their audience by abrupt and unprepared changes. The systems which governed such relations, which dictated the accepted treatment of color or chord or image, and which made the elements understandable to contemporary audiences—all were consistently broken. However, it was by breaking them, by shattering the accepted frames of reference, that the Mannerist expressed his emotion. It is for this reason that, unlike the Baroque artist, he broke with Renaissance principles without attempting to sub-

2. Mannerist drama brings out this quality very well, as is shown in *The Duchess of Malfi* by Webster.

stitute a new system of his own. Whereas both the Baroque and the Renaissance artist worked within and by means of certain established patterns, the common ground between artist and audience, Mannerism expressed itself outside of conventional forms, by deliberately shattering them, by destroying that common ground.

Without these generally accepted models the problem of structure becomes vital. Each of the works we have studied shows a strong tendency to break into parts because there are no obvious patterns left to hold it together. There seems to be no order inherent in the materials themselves; instead we get an impression of the artist struggling against the elements of his art, trying to establish a pattern among parts which refuse to give up their identity, which conflict with each other in spite of the artist, parts which exist in a condition of tension one with the other. This tension is unresolved and nondirectional. Like the dissonances in Gesualdo's madrigal, it does not lead to a resolution; it does not lead anywhere, but, for the first time, exists for its own sake. This more than anything else defines Mannerism: tension is created not to be resolved but to remain. In terms of either the Renaissance or the Baroque, the art of Gesualdo, Pontormo, Rosso, and Donne is disturbing because it is aesthetically unresolved.

The structure that does exist is a precarious balance which the mind forces upon the parts. If we look at Donne's conceits, for example, we find that the link between the tenor and the vehicle is never an obvious one, lying in the easily accessible world of common reason or the everyday realm of the senses. The key to the conceit involves the intuitive perception through ingenuity and intellect of hitherto unnoticed resemblances. Moreover, because the conceit is not always philosophically consistent with the theme of the poem, this relationship is more ingenious and formal than natural or organic.

Donne's conceit gives us an important clue to the Mannerist concept of structure as a whole. In none of the works we have been considering is the structure immediately obvious, for most of the usual devices for ordering the work of art have been ignored. In each case architectonic elements that structure the work for the audience have been avoided or underplayed.

77

In contrast to the Baroque, for example, there are very few repeated elements, such as refrains or *da capo* sections. In describing the façade of Collegio Romano, an example of Mannerist architecture by Ammanati, Nikolaus Pevsner observed that, because there is a total lack of any dominant element, the eye cannot understand or read the structure underlying the many columns.[3] The eye or ear cannot impose its own order when presented with too many unordered elements of which none stand forth to serve as center. "Unreadable" is an accurate term to describe Mannerist structure, because it is more obvious to the mind than it is to the eye or the ear. It is a structure which always emerges when a work is studied, but is seldom obvious because of the complication and refinement of the very elements which constitute it. Only those sensitive to this type of structure can perceive it.

Such a concept of structure is clearly different from that of either the Renaissance or the Baroque. Renaissance works are characterized by an essentially static or stable structure made up of clearly articulated parts which balance each other in the composition of the work. There are no opposing forces set up, and the result is a characteristic serenity and balance. The unresolved tension in Mannerism destroys this stability and serenity. A balance is always struck, but it is a precarious balance, fraught with potential disturbance. At the same time, there is none of the obvious directional pull which is common to Baroque art. The eye or ear is not drawn irresistibly in one direction, but is simultaneously pulled in several by a kind of compositional ambiguity. There are no climaxes to serve as a focus for the surrounding elements as there are in the Baroque works we have studied. Mannerism is characterized by a lack of focus, a condition of unstable equilibrium. The result is that the eye or ear remains in ceaseless but apparently aimless motion, and a feeling of seasickness, as Alfred Einstein called it, is the result.

We must not, however, suppose that, because the structure is not obvious, it is weak. On the contrary, the formal pattern is emphasized by the fact that it stands alone against a dry, art-

3. Nikolaus Pevsner, "The Architecture of Mannerism," in *The Mint* (London, Routledge and Sons, 1946), p. 132.

less, orderless nature. The glory of the Mannerist artist is that he has succeeded in creating from his mind a pattern which does not transform nature, but orders it without changing it. Since he finds nature by itself unordered and chaotic, only his own style is sincere for him, since it reveals truth as he experiences it.

It is paradoxical, therefore, that the Mannerist artists were essentially backward-looking. Donne, Pontormo, Gesualdo, and Rosso were all acutely aware of the past. Their art can only be understood in the context of the Renaissance, because a large part of its force lies in the shattering of the serenity derived from Renaissance rules or systems. Without a knowledge of these rules, the observer cannot understand Mannerist art.[4]

Historical fact underlines this Mannerist preoccupation with the past. Each of the artists we have been studying lived at a place where civilization was on the decline. Florence of the 1520s and Jacobean England both looked back with envy upon their immediate past. Most striking of all Mannerist scenes is that of Carlo Gesualdo wandering through the silent and decaying gardens of the once brilliant court of Ferrara after the death of Duke Alphonso II.

In terms of the theory of art outlined in the Introduction, the justification for the use of the term Mannerism must lie in the parallel aesthetic experiences of a number of artists living at different times and in different places. This similarity is manifested in a recognizable style which itself reflects a mood or set of commonly held metaphysical presuppositions. Many of the major elements of the mood of Mannerism have already been hinted at. Before drawing our final conclusions, however, we should examine an explicit statement presently before us of the Mannerist world view. *The First Anniversary,* John Donne's "Anatomie of the World," is of central importance to Mannerism in content as well as in style.

Donne inherited a unified view of the universe, a hierarchical vision based mainly on the Thomistic synthesis. Put into visual

4. This observation could be made about almost any new style, but applies particularly to Mannerism because the Mannerists were so self-conscious of their past, as shown by their frequent quotations from or parodies of Renaissance artists.

terms by Raphael in the Stanza della Segnatura, it held that the universe had a purpose and that man was its focal point.[5] Moreover, such a universe was essentially one, for the same principles and even the same features were to be found in the little world of man, in the earth itself, and in the heavens. Both the matter and the spirit of the universe were governed by universal rules. This view was the basis for Medieval-Renaissance theories about the laws governing the heavens, the earth, and man. Any alteration in the complex system would introduce discord in the whole, because a change in any part would, by the theory of correspondences, have repercussions in all the parts, and thus destroy the perfection of the scheme. Such an alteration was produced for Donne by the "New Philosophy," a term which was in general used to describe the empirical approach to the natural sciences. In the broadest sense, the death of Elizabeth Drury symbolizes the passing of a world order, the destruction of the old synthesis in the face of new and disrupting currents of thought.[6]

For some men, Baconians all, the New Philosophy was a cause for exhilarated optimism. For them vast spaces had been opened up, both physical and intellectual:

> The more imagination strove to grasp the astounding new universe, the more truly man realized his own potentialities, and the vaster his soul grew with that "too much" that was not enough.[7]

The First Anniversary, however, projects a view of man very different from this boisterous optimism. The earth has been corrupted in every part; man, earth, and heaven are all afflicted. We are left in a kind of twilight zone where the idea of perfection is only a ghost, barely influencing the material world:

> For there's a kind of world remaining still,
> Though shee which did inanimate and fill
> The world, be gone, yet in this last long night

5. Charles Monroe Coffin, *John Donne and the New Philosophy* (New York, Columbia University Press, 1937), p. 48.

6. Hiram Haydn, *The Counter-Renaissance* (New York, Grove Press, 1960), p. 544.

7. Nicolson, *The Breaking of the Circle*, p. 180.

> Her Ghost doth walke; that is, a glimmering light,
> A faint weake love of vertue and of good

Man in this world can only vaguely understand the material around him, because the ideal in nature has almost disappeared. The resulting vision is that of a material world fragmented, out of joint, "crumbled out againe to his Atomies." The entire poem expands the fundamental ideas of fragmentation and imperfection:

> 'Tis all in pieces, all cohaerence gone,
> All iust supply, and all Relation:

Clay Hunt sums up Donne's world view:

> The philosophic imaginations of Shakespeare and Milton tended to see the natural state of both the great world and the little world of man as one of inner harmony and peace, but Donne's mind found it more congenial to regard the natural condition of the universe, and the natural state of man, as one of disunity and precarious balance between components which were inherently disharmonious.[8]

This summary of Donne's metaphysics coincides exactly not only with the style of *The First Anniversary* but also with the style of the two *Depositions,* and of *Io parto.* Over and over again we have noted the essential acentricity or disunity of these works of art, and have remarked at the "precarious balance between components which were inherently disharmonious." The language of the style is clear, and its meaning is roughly the same in each instance. The world is in essence disunified, for there are no common laws or correspondences to bind the "pieces" together. Any order that exists is one of precarious balance imposed by man's ingenuity. This order is fragile, liable to destruction at the slightest movement, because the real is different from the ideal, because the events or parts have an existence of their own antagonistic to the order imposed. It is at least partially true that Mannerism is the result of a Renaissance aesthetic of balance and order in the mind of man confronted with the view of an external world which is chaotic

8. *Donne's Poetry,* p. 184.

81

and disunified. Each of these works represents an uneasy but somehow valiant solution to this basic conflict. Mannerist art is thus not physically but metaphysically realistic.

The only order in the universe outside of God exists in man's creative, intuitive intellect. For the Mannerist, however, man is incapable of dominating hostile nature, of recreating his own order in it. The pattern he imposes is a pattern of wit and cleverness which is in constant conflict with the material world, and this conflict is plainly manifested in the Mannerist style. The resulting mood is a distinct entity, fundamentally opposed to the moods of the surrounding ages. It is a significant commentary on the modern age that we feel we have much in common with the mood of Pontormo, Rosso, Gesualdo, and Donne, and can therefore for the first time begin to understand their style.

APPENDIX I: MUSIC AND
CADENCE CHARTS

Quando lieta sperai

RISM 1548[10], No. 12

Si ch'io vorrei morire

1) Nell'originale:

Io parto

A. CADENCE CHART [1] FOR CIPRIANO DA RORE'S *QUANDO LIETA SPERAI*

Measure Number	Root of Final Chord	Type of Cadence Authentic (V-I)	Plagal (IV-I)	Other
5	A	X		
9–10	A	X		
13–14	C	X		
15–16	C			X *
19–20	A	X		
29–30	A	X		
33–34	A			X *
36–37	E			X
38–39	E		X	
43	E			X (Phrygian)
46–47	E		X	
50–51	A	X		
56–57	E			X
63–64	A			X *
66–67	A	X		
68–69	A		X	
74–75	A		X	
80–81	A	X		
83–84	A		X	

* These cadences are all the same; they consist of a dominant seventh with the root unstated, followed by the tonic.

Total Cadences Considered:	19
Total Cadences on A:	12
Total Cadences on E:	5
Total Cadences on C:	2
Total Authentic Cadences:	8
Total Plagal Cadences:	5
Other:	6

1. In Cipriano, any cadence for two or more voices has been considered. In Monteverdi and Gesualdo, the selection has been more arbitrary, but the cadences chosen have usually been for all those voices sounding at the time.

B. CADENCE CHART FOR MONTEVERDI'S
SI CH'IO VORREI MORIRE

Measure Number	Root of Final Chord	Type of Cadence Authentic (V-I)	Plagal (IV-I)	Other
1–2	D	X		
3	A	X		
5–6	A	X		
9–10	G		X	
14–15	A	X		
35–6–7	A	X (repeated cadence with dominant seventh)		
43–44	A			X
47–48	C	X		
57–58	C	X		
63–64	A			X
73	A	X		
76–77	C	X		
78	C	X		
79–80	D	X		
81	A	X (repeat of 1st 7 measures)		
84–85	A	X		

Total Cadences: 16
Total Cadences on A: 9
Total Cadences on D: 2
Total Cadences on C: 4
Total Cadences on G: 1

Total Cadences: 16
Total Authentic Cadences: 13
Total Plagal Cadences: 1
Other: 2

C. CADENCE CHART FOR CARLO GESUALDO'S *IO PARTO*

Measure Number	Root of Final Chord	Authentic	Plagal	By Thirds	Other
3	B		X		
6	F♯		X		
11	G	X			
15	E			X	
16	A	X			
20–21	C♯				X
22	F♯			X	
24	E			X	
25–26	B			X	
28–29	B♭	X			
29–30	E			X	
32–33	E	X			
36–37	A		X(?)		X(?)
39–40	G	X			
41–42	F♯				X
43–44–45	E				X

Table header spanning: "Type of Cadence" over Authentic, Plagal, By Thirds, Other.

Total Cadences Considered: 16   Total Authentic Cadences: 4
Total Cadences on E: 5   Total Plagal Cadences: 3
Total Cadences on A or B: 4   Total Cadences by Thirds: 5
Other: 7   Other: 4

APPENDIX II: POEMS

Edmund Spenser

S *hepheards that wont on pipes of oaten reed,*
  Oft times to plaine your loves concealed smart:
And with your piteous layes have learnd to breed
Compassion in a countrey lasses hart.
Hearken ye gentle shepheards to my song,
And place my dolefull plaint your plaints emong.

To you alone I sing this mournfull verse,
The mournfulst verse that ever man heard tell:
To you whose softened hearts it may empierse,
With dolours dart for death of Astrophel.   10
To you I sing and to none other wight,
For well I wot my rymes bene rudely dight.

Yet as they been, if any nycer wit
Shall hap to heare, or covet them to read:
Thinke he, that such are for such ones most fit,
Made not to please the living but the dead.
And if in him found pity ever place,
Let him be moov'd to pity such a case.

A Gentle Shepheard borne in *Arcady*,
Of gentlest race that ever shepheard bore:
About the grassie bancks of *Hæmony*,
Did keepe his sheep, his litle stock and store.
Full carefully he kept them day and night,
In fairest fields, and *Astrophel* he hight.

Young *Astrophel* the pride of shepheards praise,
Young *Astrophel* the rusticke lasses love:
Far passing all the pastors of his daies,
In all that seemly shepheard might behove.   10
In one thing onely fayling of the best,
That he was not so happie as the rest.

For from the time that first the Nymph his mother
Him forth did bring, and taught her lambs to feed:
A sclender swaine excelling far each other,
In comely shape, like her that did him breed,
He grew up fast in goodnesse and in grace,
And doubly faire wox both in mynd and face.

Which daily more and more he did augment,
With gentle usage and demeanure myld: 20
That all mens hearts with secret ravishment
He stole away, and weetingly beguyld.
Ne spight it selfe that all good things doth spill,
Found ought in him, that she could say was ill.

His sports were faire, his ioyance innocent,
Sweet without sowre, and honny without gall:
And he himselfe seemd made for meriment,
Merily masking both in bowre and hall.
There was no pleasure nor delightfull play,
When *Astrophel* so ever was away.   30

For he could pipe and daunce, and caroll sweet,
Emongst the shepheards in their shearing feast:
As Somers larke that with her song doth greet

106

The dawning day forth comming from the East.
And layes of love he also could compose,
Thrise happie she, whom he to praise did chose.

Full many Maydens often did him woo,
Them to vouchsafe emongst his rimes to name,
Or make for them as he was wont to doo,
For her that did his heart with love inflame.
For which they promised to dight for him,
Gay chapelets of flowers and gyrlonds trim.

And many a Nymph both of the wood and brooke,
Soone as his oaten pipe began to shrill:
Both christall wells and shadie groves forsooke,
To heare the charmes of his enchanting skill.
And brought him presents, flowers if it were prime,
Or mellow fruit if it were harvest time.

But he for none of them did care a whit,
Yet wood Gods for them often sighed sore:
Ne for their gifts unworthie of his wit,
Yet not unworthie of the countries store.
For one alone he cared, for one he sight,
His lifes desire, and his deare loves delight.

Stella the faire, the fairest star in skie,
As faire as *Venus* or the fairest faire:
A fairer star saw never living eie,
Shot her sharp pointed beames through purest aire.
Her he did love, her he alone did honor,
His thoughts, his rimes, his songs were all upon her.

To her he vowd the service of his daies,
On her he spent the riches of his wit:
For her he made hymnes of immortall praise,
Of onely her he sung, he thought, he writ.
Her, and but her of love he worthie deemed,
For all the rest but litle he esteemed.

40

50

60

107

Ne her with ydle words alone he wowed,
And verses vaine (yet verses are not vaine)
But with brave deeds to her sole service vowed,
And bold atchievements her did entertaine.   70
For both in deeds and words he nourtred was,
Both wise and hardie (too hardie alas).

In wrestling nimble, and in renning swift,
In shooting steddie, and in swimming strong.
Well made to strike, to throw, to leape, to lift,
And all the sports that shepheards are emong.
In every one he vanquisht every one,
He vanquisht all, and vanquisht was of none.

Besides, in hunting such felicitie,
Or rather infelicitie he found: 80
That every field and forest far away,
He sought, where salvage beasts do most abound.
No beast so salvage but he could it kill,
No chace so hard, but he therein had skill.

Such skill matcht with such courage as he had,
Did prick him foorth with proud desire of praise:
To seek abroad, of daunger nought y'drad,
His mistresse name, and his owne fame to raise.
What needeth perill to be sought abroad,
Since round about us, it doth make aboad?   90

It fortuned, as he that perilous game
In forreine soyle pursued far away:
Into a forest wide and waste he came
Where store he heard to be of salvage pray.
So wide a forest and so waste as this,
Nor famous *Ardeyn*, nor fowle *Arlo* is.

There his welwoven toyles and subtil traines,
He laid the brutish nation to enwrap:
So well he wrought with practise and with paines,

108

That he of them great troups did soone entrap.   100
Full happie man (misweening much) was hee,
So rich a spoile within his power to see.

Eftsoones all heedlesse of his dearest hale,
Full greedily into the heard he thrust:
To slaughter them, and worke their finall bale,
Least that his toyle should of their troups be brust.
Wide wounds emongst them many one he made,
Now with his sharp borespear, now with his blade.

His care was all how he them all might kill,
That none might scape (so partiall unto none)   110
Ill mynd so much to mynd anothers ill,
As to become unmyndfull of his owne.
But pardon that unto the cruell skies,
That from himselfe to them withdrew his eies.

So as he rag'd emongst that beastly rout,
A cruell beast of most accursed brood
Upon him turnd (despeyre makes cowards stout)
And with fell tooth accustomed to blood,
Launched his thigh with so mischievous might,
That it both bone and muscles ryved quight.   120

So deadly was the dint and deep the wound,
And so huge streames of blood thererout did flow:
That he endured not the direfull stound,
But on the cold deare earth himselfe did throw.
The whiles the captive heard his nets did rend,
And having none to let, to wood did wend.

Ah where were ye this while his shepheard peares,
To whom alive was nought so deare as hee:
And ye faire Mayds the matches of his yeares,
Which in his grace did boast you most to bee?   130
Ah where were ye, when he of you had need,
To stop his wound that wondrously did bleed?

Ah wretched boy the shape of dreryhead,
And sad ensample of mans suddein end:
Full litle faileth but thou shalt be dead,
Unpitied, unplaynd, of foe or frend.
Whilest none is nigh, thine eylids up to close,
And kisse thy lips like faded leaves of rose.

A sort of shepheards sewing of the chace,
As they the forest raunged on a day: 140
By fate or fortune came unto the place,
Where as the lucklesse boy yet bleeding lay.
Yet bleeding lay, and yet would still have bled,
Had not good hap those shepheards thether led.

They stopt his wound (too late to stop it was)
And in their armes then softly did him reare:
Tho (as he wild) unto his loved lasse,
His dearest love him dolefully did beare.
The dolefulst beare that ever man did see,
Was *Astrophel*, but dearest unto mee.   150

She when she saw her love in such a plight,
With crudled blood and filthie gore deformed:
That wont to be with flowers and gyrlonds dight,
And her deare favours dearly well adorned,
Her face, the fairest face, that eye mote see,
She likewise did deforme like him to bee.

Her yellow locks that shone so bright and long,
As Sunny beames in fairest somers day:
She fiersly tore, and with outragious wrong
From her red cheeks the roses rent away.   160
And her faire brest the threasury of ioy,
She spoyld thereof, and filled with annoy.

His palled face impictured with death,
She bathed oft with teares and dried oft:
And with sweet kisses suckt the wasting breath,
Out of his lips like lillies pale and soft.

110

And oft she cald to him, who answerd nought,
But onely by his lookes did tell his thought.

The rest of her impatient regret,
And piteous mone the which she for him made: 170
No toong can tell, nor any forth can set,
But he whose heart like sorrow did invade.
At last when paine his vitall powres had spent,
His wasted life her weary lodge forwent.

Which when she saw, she staied not a whit,
But after him did make untimely haste:
Forth with her ghost out of her corps did flit,
And followed her make like Turtle chaste.
To prove that death their hearts cannot divide,
Which living were in love so firmly tide.   180

The Gods which all things see, this same beheld,
And pittying this paire of lovers trew:
Transformed them there lying on the field,
Into one flowre that is both red and blew.
It first growes red, and then to blew doth fade,
Like *Astrophel*, which thereinto was made.

And in the midst thereof a star appeares,
As fairly formd as any star in skyes:
Resembling *Stella* in her freshest yeares,
Forth darting beames of beautie from her eyes,   190
And all the day it standeth full of deow,
Which is the teares, that from her eyes did flow.

That hearbe of some, Starlight is cald by name,
Of others *Penthia*, though not so well:
But thou where ever thou doest finde the same,
From this day forth do call it *Astrophel*.
And when so ever thou it up doest take,
Do pluck it softly for that shepheards sake.

Hereof when tydings far abroad did passe,
The shepheards all which loved him full deare,   200
And sure full deare of all he loved was,
Did thether flock to see what they did heare.
And when that pitteous spectacle they vewed,
The same with bitter teares they all bedewed.

And every one did make exceeding mone,
With inward anguish and great griefe opprest:
And every one did weep and waile, and mone,
And meanes deviz'd to shew his sorrow best.
That from that houre since first on grassie greene,
Shepheards kept sheep, was not like mourning seen.   210

But first his sister that *Clorinda* hight,
The gentlest shepheardesse that lives this day:
And most resembling both in shape and spright
Her brother deare, began this dolefull lay.
Which least I marre the sweetnesse of the vearse,
In sort as she it sung, I will rehearse.

Dolefull Lay of Clorinda

AY me, to whom shall I my case complaine,
That may compassion my impatient griefe?
Or where shall I unfold my inward paine,
That my enriven heart may find reliefe?
Shall I unto the heavenly powres it show?
Or unto earthly men that dwell below?

To heavens? ah they alas the authors were,
And workers of my unremedied wo:
For they foresee what to us happens here,
And they foresaw, yet suffred this be so.   10
    From them comes good, from them comes also il,
    That which they made, who can them warne to spill.

To men? ah they alas like wretched bee,
And subiect to the heavens ordinance:
Bound to abide what ever they decree,
Their best redresse, is their best sufferance.
    How then can they like wretched comfort mee,
    The which no lesse, need comforted to bee?

Then to my selfe will I my sorrow mourne,
Sith none alive like sorrowfull remaines: 20
And to my selfe my plaints shall back retourne,
To pay their usury with doubled paines.
    The woods, the hills, the rivers shall resound
    The mournful accent of my sorrowes ground.

Woods, hills and rivers, now are desolate,
Sith he is gone the which them all did grace:
And all the fields do waile their widow state,
Sith death their fairest flowre did late deface.
    The fairest flowre in field that ever grew,
    Was *Astrophel;* that was, we all may rew.   30

What cruell hand of cursed foe unknowne,
Hath cropt the stalke which bore so faire a flowre?

113

Untimely cropt, before it well were growne,
And cleane defaced in untimely howre.
  Great losse to all that ever him did see,
  Great losse to all, but greatest losse to mee.

Breake now your gyrlonds, O ye shepheards lasses,
Sith the faire flowre, which them adornd, is gon:
The flowre, which them adornd, is gone to ashes,
Never againe let lasse put gyrlond on.   40
  In stead of gyrlond, weare sad Cypres nowe,
  And bitter Elder, broken from the bowe.

Ne ever sing the love-layes which he made,
Who ever made such layes of love as hee?
Ne ever read the riddles, which he sayd
Unto your selves, to make you mery glee.
  Your mery glee is now laid all abed,
  Your mery maker now alasse is dead.

Death the devourer of all worlds delight,
Hath robbed you and reft fro me my ioy: 50
Both you and me, and all the world he quight
Hath robd of ioyance, and left sad annoy.
  Ioy of the world, and shepheards pride was hee,
  Shepheards hope never like againe to see.

Oh death that hast us of such riches reft,
Tell us at least, what hast thou with it done?
What is become of him whose flowre here left
Is but the shadow of his likenesse gone.
  Scarse like the shadow of that which he was,
  Nought like, but that he like a shade did pas.   60

But that immortall spirit, which was deckt
With all the dowries of celestiall grace:
By soveraine choyce from th'hevenly quires select,
And lineally deriv'd from Angels race,
  O what is now of it become aread.
  Ay me, can so divine a thing be dead?

114

Ah no: it is not dead, ne can it die,
But lives for aie, in blisfull Paradise:
Where like a new-borne babe it soft doth lie,
In bed of lillies wrapt in tender wise.   70
   And compast all about with roses sweet,
   And daintie violets from head to feet.

There thousand birds all of celestiall brood,
To him do sweetly caroll day and night:
And with straunge notes, of him well understood,
Lull him a sleep in Angelick delight;
   Whilest in sweet dreame to him presented bee
   Immortall beauties, which no eye may see.

But he them sees and takes exceeding pleasure
Of their divine aspects, appearing plaine,   80
And kindling love in him above all measure,
Sweet love still ioyous, never feeling paine.
   For what so goodly forme he there doth see,
   He may enioy from iealous rancor free.

There liveth he in everlasting blis,
Sweet spirit never fearing more to die:
Ne dreading harme from any foes of his,
Ne fearing salvage beasts more crueltie.
   Whilest we here wretches waile his private lack,
   And with vaine vowes do often call him back.   90

But live thou there still happie, happie spirit,
And give us leave thee here thus to lament:
Not thee that doest thy heavens ioy inherit,
But our owne selves that here in dole are drent.
   Thus do we weep and waile, and wear our eies,
   Mourning in others, our owne miseries.

Which when she ended had, another swaine
Of gentle wit and daintie sweet device:
Whom *Astrophel* full deare did entertaine,
Whilest here he liv'd, and held in passing price,   100

115

Hight *Thestylis,* began his mournfull tourne,
And made the *Muses* in his song to mourne.

And after him full many other moe,
As everie one in order lov'd him best,
Gan dight themselves t'expresse their inward woe,
With dolefull layes unto the time addrest.
The which I here in order will rehearse,
As fittest flowres to deck his mournfull hearse.

Richard Crashaw

H ark! she is call'd, the parting houre is come.
⎯ Take thy farewell, poore world! Heav'n must goe home.
A peece of Heav'nly Earth, purer and brighter
Than the chast stars, whose choice lamps come to light her,
While through the Christall orbes, clearer than they,   5
She climbs; and makes a farre more milky way.
She's call'd. Harke how the deare immortall *Dove*
Sighes to his silver mate. *Rise up my Love,*
    Rise up my faire, my spotlesse one,
    The winters past, the Rain is gone: 10
    The spring is come, the Flowers appeare,
    No sweets but thou are wanting here.
          Come away my love,
          Come away my dove,
              Cast off delay: 15
       The Court of Heav'n is come,
       To waite upon thee home;
          Come, come away.
      ⎯⎯⎯⎯⎯ The Flowers appeare,
    Or quickly would, were thou once here.   20
    The spring is come; Or if it stay,
    'Tis to keepe time with thy delay.
The raine is gone, Except as much as wee,
Detain in needfull *Teares,* to weep the want of thee.
          ⎯⎯⎯ The winters past,   25
       Or if he make lesse haste,
       His answer is, Why, she doth so;
If summer come not, how can winter go?
       Come away, come away,
The shrill winds chide, the waters weep thy stay,   30
The fountaines murmure; and each loftiest Tree,
Bowes lowest his leavy top, to looke for thee.
       Come away my love,
       Come away my dove, &c.
She's call'd again; And will she goe?   35
When Heav'n bids come, who can say No?

117

Heav'n calls her, and she must away,
Heav'n will not, and she cannot stay.
Goe then, goe (*glorious*) on the golden wings
Of the bright youth of Heav'n that sings   40
Under so sweet a burden, *Goe,*
Since thy dread *Son* will have it so.
And while thou goest, our Song and wee,
Will as wee may reach after thee.
    Haile, holy Queen, of humble Hearts!   45
    We in thy praise wil have our parts.
And though thy dearest lookes must now be light
To none but the blest heavens, whose bright
Beholders lost in sweet delight,
Feed for ever their faire sight   50
With those divinest eyes, which wee
And our darke world no more shall see;
Though our poore joyes are parted so,
Yet shall our lips never let goe
Thy gracious name, but to the last   55
Our loving song shall hold it fast.
    Thy precious Name shall bee
    Thy self to us, and wee
    With holy care will keep it by us.
      Wee to the last   60
      Will hold it fast;
    And no Assumption shall deny us.
      All the sweetest showers
      Of our fairest flowers,
    Will wee strow upon it;   65
      Though our sweets cannot make
      It sweeter, they can take
    Themselves new sweetnesse from it.
  Maria, Men and Angels sing,
  Maria, Mother of our King.   70
Live, Rosie Princesse, live, and may the bright
Crowne of a most incomparable light
Embrace thy radiant browes: O may the best
Of everlasting joyes bath thy white brest.
    Live our chaste love, the holy mirth   75

118

Of heav'n, the Humble pride of Earth.
Live, crowne of women, Queen of men;
Live Mistrisse of our Song; And when
Our weake desires have done their best,
Sweet Angels come, and sing the Rest.   80

John Donne

THE FIRST ANNIVERSARY.

AN

ANATOMY OF

THE WORLD.

W hen that rich soule which to her Heaven
    is gone,   *The entrie*
Whom all they celebrate, who know they have one,   *into the*
(For who is sure he hath a soule, unlesse   *worke.*
It see, and Iudge, and follow worthinesse,
And by Deedes praise it? He who doth not this,   5
May lodge an In-mate soule, but tis not his.)
When that Queene ended here her progresse time,
And, as t'her standing house, to heaven did clymbe,
Where, loth to make the Saints attend her long,
Shee's now a part both of the Quire, and Song,   10
This world, in that great earth-quake languished;
For in a common Bath of teares it bled,
Which drew the strongest vitall spirits out:
But succour'd then with a perplexed doubt,
Whether the world did loose or gaine in this,   15
(Because since now no other way there is
But goodnes, to see her, whom all would see,
All must endevour to be good as shee,)
This great consumption to a fever turn'd,
And so the world had fits; it ioy'd, it mournd.   20
And, as men thinke, that Agues physicke are,
And th'Ague being spent, give over care,
So thou, sicke world, mistak'st thy selfe to bee
Well, when alas, thou'rt in a Letargee.
Her death did wound, and tame thee than, and than   25
Thou mightst have better spar'd the Sunne, or Man;
That wound was deepe, but 'tis more misery,
That thou hast lost thy sense and memory.
T'was heavy then to heare thy voyce of mone,
But this is worse, that thou art speechlesse growne.   30

120

Thou hast forgot thy name, thou hadst; thou wast
Nothing but she, and her thou hast o'repast.
For as a child kept from the Font, untill
A Prince, expected long, come to fulfill
The Ceremonies, thou unnam'd hadst laid,   35
Had not her comming, thee her Palace made:
Her name defin'd thee, gave thee forme and frame,
And thou forgetst to celebrate thy name.
Some moneths she hath beene dead (but being dead,
Measures of times are all determined)   40
But long shee'ath beene away, long, long, yet none
Offers to tell us who it is that's gone.
But as in states doubtfull of future heyres,
When sickenes without remedy, empayres
The present Prince, they're loth it should be said,   45
The Prince doth languish, or the Prince is dead:
So mankind feeling now a generall thaw,
A strong example gone equall to law,
The Cyment which did faithfully compact
And glue all vertues, now resolv'd, and slack'd,   50
Thought it some blasphemy to say sh'was dead;
Or that our weakenes was discovered
In that confession; therefore spoke no more
Then tongues, the soule being gone, the losse deplore.
But though it be too late to succour thee,   55
Sicke world, yea dead, yea putrified, since shee
Thy'ntrinsique Balme, and thy preservative,
Can never be renew'd, thou never live,
I (since no man can make thee live) will trie,
What we may gaine by thy Anatomy.   60
Her death hath taught us dearely, that thou art
Corrupt and mortall in thy purest part.
Let no man say, the world it selfe being dead,
'Tis labour lost to have discovered
The worlds infirmities, since there is none   65
Alive to study this dissectione;
For there's a kind of world remaining still,   *What life*
Though shee which did inanimate and fill   *the world*
The world, be gone, yet in this last long night,   *hath still*

121

Her Ghost doth walke; that is, a glimmering light,   70
A faint weake love of vertue and of good
Reflects from her, on them which understood
Her worth; And though she have shut in all day,
The twi-light of her memory doth stay;
Which, from the carcasse of the old world, free,   75
Creates a new world; and new creatures be
Produc'd: The matter and the stuffe of this,
Her vertue, and the forme our practise is.
And though to be thus Elemented, arme
These Creatures, from hom-borne intrinsique harme,   80
(For all assum'd unto this Dignitee,
So many weedlesse Paradises bee,
Which of themselves produce no venemous sinne,
Except some forraine Serpent bring it in)
Yet, because outward stormes the strongest breake,   85
And strength it selfe by confidence growes weake,
This new world may be safer, being told
The dangers and disease of the old: *The sicknesses of the world.*
For with due temper men do then forgoe,
Or covet things, when they their true worth know.   90
There is no health; Physitians say that we   *Impossibility of health.*
At best, enjoy, but a neutralitee.
And can there be worse sickenesse, then to know
That we are never well, nor can be so?
We are borne ruinous: poore mothers crie,   95
That children come not right, nor orderly,
Except they headlong come, and fall upon
An ominous precipitation.
How witty's ruine? how importunate
Upon mankinde? It labour'd to frustrate   100
Even Gods purpose; and made woman, sent
For mans reliefe, cause of his languishment.
They were to good ends, and they are so still,
But accessory, and principall in ill.
For that first mariage was our funerall: 105
One woman at one blow, then kill'd us all,
And singly, one by one, they kill us now.
We doe delightfully our selves allow

122

To that consumption; and profusely blinde,
We kill our selves, to propagate our kinde. 110
And yet we doe not that; we are not men:
There is not now that mankinde, which was then
When as the Sunne, and man, did seeme to strive,
(Ioynt tenants of the world) who should survive. *Shortnesse*
When Stag, and Raven, and the long-liv'd tree, *of life.* 115
Compar'd with man, dy'de in minoritee.
When, if a slow-pac'd starre had stolne away
From the observers marking, he might stay
Two or three hundred yeares to see't againe,
And then make up his observation plaine; 120
When, as the age was long, the sise was great:
Mans grouth confess'd, and recompenc'd the meat:
So spacious and large, that every soule
Did a faire Kingdome, and large Realme controule:
And when the very stature thus erect, 125
Did that soule a good way towards Heaven direct.
Where is this mankind now? who lives to age,
Fit to be made *Methusalem* his page?
Alas, we scarse live long enough to trie
Whether a new made clocke runne right, or lie. 130
Old Grandsires talke of yesterday with sorrow,
And for our children we reserve to morrow.
So short is life, that every peasant strives,
In a torne house, or field, to have three lives.
And as in lasting, so in length is man 135
Contracted to an inch, who was a span. *Smalenesse*
For had a man at first, in Forrests stray'd, *of stature.*
Or shipwrack'd in the Sea, one would have laid
A wager that an Elephant, or Whale
That met him, would not hastily assaile 140
A thing so equall to him: now alas,
The Fayries, and the Pigmies well may passe
As credible; mankind decayes so soone,
We're scarse our Fathers shadowes cast at noone.
Onely death addes t'our length: nor are we growne 145
In stature to be men, till we are none.
But this were light, did our less volume hold

All the old Text; or had we chang'd to gold
Their silver; or dispos'd into lesse glas,
Spirits of vertue, which then scattred was.   150
But 'tis not so: w'are not retir'd, but dampt;
And as our bodies, so our mindes are cramp't:
'Tis shrinking, not close-weaving, that hath thus,
In minde and body both bedwarfed us.
We seeme ambitious, Gods whole worke t'undoe;   155
Of nothing he made us, and we strive too,
To bring our selves to nothing backe; and we
Do what we can, to do't so soone as hee.
With new diseases on our selves we warre,
And with new phisicke, a worse Engin farre.   160
Thus man, this worlds Vice-Emperor, in whom
All faculties, all graces are at home;
And if in other Creatures they appeare,
They're but mans ministers, and Legats there,
To worke on their rebellions, and reduce   165
Them to Civility, and to mans use.
This man, whom God did wooe, and loth t'attend
Till man came up, did downe to man descend,
This man, so great, that all that is, is his,
Oh what a trifle, and poore thing he is!   170
If man were any thing, he's nothing now:
Helpe, or at least some time to wast, allow
T'his other wants, yet when he did depart
With her, whom we lament, he lost his hart.
She, of whom th'Auncients seem'd to prophesie,   175
When they call'd vertues by the name of shee,
She in whom vertue was so much refin'd,
That for Allay unto so pure a minde
Shee tooke the weaker Sex, she that could drive
The poysonous tincture, and the stayne of *Eve*,   180
Out of her thoughts, and deeds; and purifie
All, by a true religious Alchimy;
Shee, shee is dead; shee's dead: when thou knowest this,
Thou knowest how poore a trifling thing man is.
And learn'st thus much by our Anatomee,   185
The heart being perish'd, no part can be free.

124

And that except thou feed (not banquet) on
The supernaturall food, Religion,
Thy better Grouth growes withered, and scant;
Be more then man, or thou'rt lesse then an Ant.   190
Then, as mankinde, so is the worlds whole frame
Quite out of ioynt, almost created lame:
For, before God had made up all the rest,
Corruption entred, and deprav'd the best:
It seis'd the Angels, and then first of all   195
The world did in her Cradle take a fall,
And turn'd her braines, and tooke a generall maime
Wronging each ioynt of th'universall frame.
The noblest part, man, felt it first; and than
Both beasts and plants, curst in the curse of man. *Decay of*   200
So did the world from the first houre decay,   *nature in*
The evening was beginning of the day,   *other parts.*
And now the Springs and Sommers which we see,
Like sonnes of women after fifty bee.
And new Philosophy cals all in doubt,   205
The Element of fire is quite put out;
The Sunne is lost, and th'earth, and no mans wit
Can well direct him, where to looke for it.
And freely men confesse, that this world's spent,
When in the Planets, and the Firmament   210
They seeke so many new; they see that this
Is crumbled out againe to his Atomis.
'Tis all in pieces, all cohaerence gone;
All iust supply, and all Relation:
Prince, Subiect, Father, Sonne, are things forgot,   215
For every man alone thinkes he hath got
To be a Phoenix, and that there can bee
None of that kinde, of which he is, but hee.
This is the worlds condition now, and now
She that should all parts to reunion bow,   220
She that had all Magnetique force alone,
To draw, and fasten sundred parts in one;
She whom wise nature had invented then
When she observ'd that every sort of men
Did in their voyage in this worlds Sea stray,   225

And needed a new compasse for their way;
Shee that was best, and first originall
Of all faire copies; and the generall
Steward to Fate; shee whose rich eyes, and brest,
Guilt the West Indies, and perfum'd the East;   230
Whose having breath'd in this world, did bestow
Spice on those Isles, and bad them still smell so,
And that rich Indie which doth gold interre,
Is but as single money, coyn'd from her:
She to whom this world must it selfe refer,   235
As Suburbs, or the Microcosme of her,
Shee, shee is dead; shee's dead: when thou knowst this,
Thou knowst how lame a cripple this world is.
And learnst thus much by our Anatomy,
That this worlds generall sickenesse doth not lie   240
In any humour, or one certaine part;
But, as thou sawest it rotten at the hart,
Thou seest a Hectique fever hath got hold
Of the whole substance, not to be contrould,
And that thou hast but one way, not t'admit   245
The worlds infection, to be none of it.
For the worlds subtilst immateriall parts
Feele this consuming wound, and ages darts.
For the worlds beauty is decayd, or gone,
Beauty, that's colour, and proportion.   *Disformity*   250
We thinke the heavens enjoy their Sphericall   *of parts.*
Their round proportion embracing all.
But yet their various and perplexed course,
Observ'd in divers ages doth enforce
Men to finde out so many Eccentrique parts,   255
Such divers downe-right lines, such overthwarts,
As disproportion that pure forme. It teares
The Firmament in eight and fortie sheeres,
And in those constellations there arise
New starres, and old do vanish from our eyes: 260
As though heav'n suffred earth-quakes, peace or war,
When new Townes rise, and olde demolish'd are.
They have empayld within a Zodiake
The free-borne Sunne, and keepe twelve signes awake
To watch his steps; the Goat and Crabbe controule,   265

126

And fright him backe, who els to eyther Pole,
(Did not these Tropiques fetter him) might runne:
For his course is not round; nor can the Sunne
Perfit a Circle, or maintaine his way
One inche direct; but where he rose to day   270
He comes no more, but with a cousening line,
Steales by that point, and so is Serpentine:
And seeming weary with his reeling thus,
He meanes to sleepe, being now falne nearer us.
So, of the stares which boast that they do runne   275
In Circle still, none ends where he begunne.
All their proportion's lame, it sinks, it swels.
For of Meridians, and Parallels,
Man hath weav'd out a net, and this net throwne
Upon the Heavens, and now they are his owne.   280
Loth to goe up the hill, or labor thus
To goe to heaven, we make heaven come to us.
We spur, we raine the stars, and in their race
They're diversly content t'obey our pace.
But keepes the earth her round proportion still?   285
Doth not a Tenarif, or higher Hill
Rise so high like a Rocke, that one might thinke
The floating Moone would shipwracke there, and sink?
Seas are so deepe, that Whales being strooke to day,
Perchance to morrow, scarse at middle way   290
Of their wish'd iourneys end, the bottom, dye.
And men, to sound depths, so much line untie,
As one might iustly thinke, that there would rise
At end thereof, one of th'Antipodies:
If under all, a Vault infernall be,   295
(Which sure is spacious, except that we
Invent another torment, that there must
Millions into a strait hote roome be thrust)
Then solidnes, and roundnes have no place.
Are these but warts, and pock-holes in the face   300
Of th'earth? Thinke so: But yet confesse, in this
The worlds proportion disfigured is,
That these two legges whereon it doth relie,   *Disorder in the*
Reward and punishment are bent awrie.   *world.*
And, Oh, it can no more be questioned,   305

127

That beauties best, proportion, is dead,
Since even griefe it selfe, which now alone
Is left us, is without proportion.
Shee by whose lines proportion should bee
Examin'd, measure of all Symmetree,   310
Whom had that Ancient seen, who thought soules made
Of Harmony, he would at next have said
That Harmony was shee, and thence infer,
That soules were but Resultances from her,
And did from her into our bodies go,   315
As to our eyes, the formes from obiects flow:
Shee, who if those great Doctors truely said
That th'Arke to mans proportions was made,
Had beene a type for that, as that might be
A type of her in this, that contrary   320
Both Elements, and Passions liv'd at peace
In her, who caus'd all Civill warre to cease.
Shee, after whom, what forme soe're we see,
Is discord, and rude incongruitee,
Shee, shee is dead, she's dead; when thou knowst this,   325
Thou knowst how ugly a monster this world is:
And learnst thus much by our Anatomee,
That here is nothing to enamor thee:
And that, not onely faults in inward parts,
Corruptions in our braines, or in our harts,   330
Poysoning the fountaines, whence our actions spring,
Endanger us: but that if every thing
Be not done fitly'nd in proportion,
To satisfie wise, and good lookers on,
(Since most men be such as most thinke they bee)   335
They're lothsome too, by this Deformitee.
For good, and well, must in our actions meete:
Wicked is not much worse then indiscreet.
But beauties other second Element,
Colour, and lustre now, is as neere spent.   340
And had the world his iust proportion,
Were it a ring still, yet the stone is gone.
As a compassionate Turcoyse which doth tell
By looking pale, the wearer is not well,

128

As gold fals sicke being stung with Mercury,   345
All the worlds parts of such complexion bee.
When nature was most busie, the first weeke,
Swadling the new-borne earth, God seemd to like,
That she should sport herselfe sometimes, and play,
To mingle, and vary colours every day.   350
And then, as though she could not make inow,
Himselfe his various Rainbow did allow.
Sight is the noblest sense of any one,
Yet sight hath onely color to feed on,
And color is decayd: summers robe growes   355
Duskie, and like an oft dyed garment showes.
Our blushing redde, which us'd in cheekes to spred,
Is inward sunke, and onely our soules are redde.
Perchance the world might have recovered,
If she whom we lament had not beene dead: 360
But shee, in whom all white, and redde, and blue
(Beauties ingredients) voluntary grew,
As in an unvext Paradise; from whom
Did all things verdure, and their lustre come,
Whose composition was miraculous,   365
Being all color, all Diaphanous,
(For Ayre, and Fire but thicke grosse bodies were,
And liveliest stones but drowsie, and pale to her,)
Shee, shee is dead; shee's dead: when thou knowst this,
Thou knowst how wan a Ghost this our world is: 370
And learnst thus much by our Anatomee,
That it should more affright, then pleasure thee.
And that, since all faire color then did sinke,
Tis now but wicked vanity to thinke,
To color vitious deeds with good pretence,   *Weaknesse*   375
Or with bought colors to illude mens sense.   *in the want of*
                                               correspondence
Nor in ought more this worlds decay appeares, *of heaven and*
Then that her influence the heav'n forbeares, *earth*
Or that the Elements doe not feele this,
The father, or the mother barren is.   380
The clouds conceive not raine, or doe not powre
In the due birth-time, downe the balmy showre.
Th'Ayre doth not motherly sit on the earth,

To hatch her seasons, and give all things birth.
Spring-times were common cradles, but are toombes;   385
And false-conceptions fill the generall wombs.
Th'Ayre showes such Meteors, as none can see,
Not onely what they meane, but what they bee.
Earth such new wormes, as would have troubled much,
Th'Egyptian Mages to have made more such.   390
What Artist now dares boast that he can bring
Heaven hither, or constellate any thing,
So as the influence of those starres may bee
Imprisond in an Herbe, or Charme, or Tree,
And doe by touch, all which those starres could do?   395
The art is lost, and correspondence too.
For heaven gives little, and the earth takes lesse,
And man least knowes their trade, and purposes.
If this commerce twixt heaven and earth were not
Embarr'd, and all this trafique quite forgot,   400
Shee, for whose losse we have lamented thus,
Would worke more fully'and pow'rfully on us.
Since herbes, and roots by dying, lose not all,
But they, yea Ashes too, are medicinall,
Death could not quench her vertue so, but that   405
It would be (if not follow'd) wondred at:
And all the world would be one dying Swan,
To sing her funerall prayse, and vanish than.
But as some Serpents poison hurteth not,
Except it be from the live Serpent shot,   410
So doth her vertue need her here, to fit
That unto us; she working more then it.
But she, in whom, to such maturity,
Vertue was growne, past growth, that it must die,
She from whose influence all Impressions came,   415
But, by Receivers impotencies, lame,
Who, though she could not transubstantiate
All states to gold, yet guilded every state,
So that some Princes have some temperance;
Some Counsaylors some purpose to advance   420
The common profite; and some people have
Some stay, no more then Kings should give, to crave;

130

Some women have some taciturnity;
Some Nunneries, some graines of chastity.
She that did thus much, and much more could doe,   425
But that our age was Iron, and rusty too,
Shee, shee is dead; shee's dead: when thou knowst this,
Thou knowest how drie a Cinder this world is.
And learnst thus much by our Anatomy,
That 'tis in vaine to dew, or mollifie   430
It with thy Teares, or Sweat, or Bloud: no thing
Is worth our travaile, griefe, or perishing,
But those rich ioyes, which did possesse her hart,
Of which shee's now partaker, and a part.
But as in cutting up a man that's dead,   *Conclusion.*   435
The body will not last out to have read
On every part, and therefore men direct
Their speech to parts, that are of most effect;
So the worlds carcasse would not last, if I
Were punctuall in this Anatomy.   440
Nor smels it well to hearers, if one tell
Them their disease, who faine would think they're wel.
Here therefore be the end: And, blessed maid,
Of whom is meant what ever hath beene said,
Or shall be spoken well by any tongue,   445
Whose name refines course lines, and makes prose song,
Accept this tribute, and his first yeares rent,
Who till his darke short tapers end be spent,
As oft as thy feast sees this widowed earth,
Will yearely celebrate thy second birth,   450
That is, thy death. For though the soule of man
Be got when man is made, 'tis borne but than
When man doth die. Our body's as the wombe,
And as a mid-wife death directs it home.
And you her creatures, whom she workes upon   455
And have your last, and best concoction
From her example, and her vertue, if you
In reverence to her, doe thinke it due,
That no one should her prayses thus reherse,
As matter fit for Chronicle, not verse,   460
Vouchsafe to call to minde, that God did make

131

A last, and lastingst peece, a song. He spake
To *Moses*, to deliver unto all,
That song: because he knew they would let fall,
The Law, the Prophets, and the History,   465
But keepe the song still in their memory.
Such an opinion (in due measure) made
Me this great Office boldly to invade.
Nor could incomprehensiblenesse deterre
Me, from thus trying to emprison her.   470
Which when I saw that a strict grave could do,
I saw not why verse might not doe so too.
Verse hath a middle nature: heaven keepes soules,
The grave keeps bodies, verse the fame enroules.

BIBLIOGRAPHY

I. General Works on Mannerism as a phenomenon in more than one art form.

Artz, Frederick B., *From the Renaissance to Romanticism*, Chicago and London, University of Chicago Press, 1962.
Hauser, Arnold, *The Social History of Art, 2*, New York, Vintage Books, 1960.
Haydn, Hiram, *The Counter-Renaissance*, New York, Grove Press, 1960.
Sypher, Wylie, *Four Stages of Renaissance Style: Transformations in Art and Literature*, Garden City, New York, Doubleday, 1955.

II. Mannerism in Painting: Pontormo and Rosso

Blunt, Anthony, *Artistic Theory in Italy, 1450–1600*, London, Oxford University Press, 1956.
Brigandi, Giuliano, *Le Maniérisme Italien*, Leipzig, VEB Edition, 1962.
Freedberg, Sydney J., *Parmigianino*, Cambridge, Harvard University Press, 1950.
Friedlaender, Walter F., *Caravaggio Studies*, Princeton, Princeton University Press, 1955.
———, *Mannerism and Anti-Mannerism in Italian Painting*, New York, Columbia University Press, 1958.
Pevsner, Nikolaus, "The Architecture of Mannerism," *The Mint*, London, Routledge and Sons, 1946.
Stokes, Adrian, *Michelangelo: A Study in the Nature of Art*, London, Tavistock Publications, 1955.
Le Triomphe du Maniérisme Européen, Exhibition catalogue, Amsterdam, Rijksmuseum, 1955.

III. Mannerism in Music: Carlo Gesualdo

Cannon, Beekman C., Alvin H. Johnson, and William G. Waite, *The Art of Music*, New York, Thomas Y. Crowell Company, 1960.

Einstein, Alfred, *The Italian Madrigal*, Princeton, Princeton University Press, 1949, 3 vols.

Gray, Cecil, and Philip Heseltine, *Carlo Gesualdo, Prince of Venosa, Musician and Murderer*, London, J. Curwen & Sons, 1926.

Lowinsky, Edward E., *Tonality and Atonality in Sixteenth Century Music*, Berkeley and Los Angeles, University of California Press, 1961.

Marshall, George Ruffin, "The Harmonic Laws in the Madrigals of Carlo Gesualdo," unpublished dissertation, New York University, December 1955.

Schrade, Leo, *Monteverdi: Creator of Modern Music*, New York, W. W. Norton & Co., 1950.

Strunk, Oliver, ed., *Source Readings in Music History*, New York, W. W. Norton & Co., 1950.

IV. Mannerism in Literature: John Donne

Coffin, Charles Monroe, *John Donne and the New Philosophy*, New York, Columbia University Press, 1937.

Hunt, Clay, *Donne's Poetry: Essays in Literary Analysis*, New Haven, Yale University Press, 1954.

Mahood, M. M., *Poetry and Humanism*, New Haven, Yale University Press, 1950.

Martz, Louis L., *The Poetry of Meditation*, New Haven, Yale University Press, 1954.

de Morques, Odette, *Metaphysical, Baroque, and Précieux Poetry*, Oxford, Clarendon Press, 1953.

Nicolson, Marjorie, *The Breaking of the Circle*, Evanston, Illinois, Northwestern University Press, 1950.

Warnke, Frank J., *European Metaphysical Poetry*, New Haven and London, Yale University Press, 1961.

Warren, Austin, *Richard Crashaw: A Study in Baroque Sensibility*, Baton Rouge, La., Louisiana State University Press, 1939.

INDEX

136